NAFTA
AND CLIMATE
CHANGE

Meera Fickling & Jeffrey J. Schott

PETERSON INSTITUTE FOR INTERNATIONAL ECONOMICS
Washington, DC

September 2011

Meera Fickling was a research analyst at the Peterson Institute from 2008 to 2011 and is now pursuing a graduate degree in environmental studies at Duke University. Her areas of research focus on climate change and trade. Among her publications are Trade and the Environment (in *Oxford Handbook on the World Trade Organization*, Oxford University Press) and two Peterson Institute policy briefs: *Revisiting the NAFTA Agenda on Climate Change* (2010) and *Setting the NAFTA Agenda on Climate Change* (2009). She graduated summa cum laude from the College of William and Mary, where she majored in economics.

Jeffrey J. Schott, senior fellow, joined the Peterson Institute in 1983. During his tenure at the Institute, he also has been a visiting lecturer at Princeton University (1994) and an adjunct professor at Georgetown University (1986–88). He was a senior associate at the Carnegie Endowment for International Peace (1982–83) and an official of the US Treasury Department (1974–82) in international trade and energy policy. He is a member of two advisory committees to the US government: the Trade and Environment Policy Advisory Committee and the Advisory Committee on International Economic Policy of the US Department of State. Schott is the author or coauthor of numerous books on trade, including *Figuring Out the Doha Round* (2010), *Economic Sanctions Reconsidered*, 3rd edition (2007), *NAFTA Revisited: Achievements and Challenges* (2005), *Free Trade Agreements: US Strategies and Priorities* (2004), *Free Trade between Korea and the United States?* (2001), *Prospects for Free Trade in the Americas* (2001), *NAFTA and the Environment: Seven Years Later* (2000), *NAFTA: An Assessment* (1993), and *North American Free Trade: Issues and Recommendations* (1992).

PETER G. PETERSON INSTITUTE FOR INTERNATIONAL ECONOMICS
1750 Massachusetts Avenue, NW
Washington, DC 20036-1903
(202) 328-9000   FAX: (202) 659-3225
www.piie.com

C. Fred Bergsten, *Director*
Edward A. Tureen, *Director of Publications, Marketing, and Web Development*

Typesetting by Susann Luetjen
Printing by Versa Press, Inc.
Cover design by Fletcher Design
Cover photos: © Iakov Kalinin, Jim Barber, klikk, and Bryan Busovicki—Fotolia

Printed in the United States of America
13   12   11   5   4   3   2   1

Library of Congress Cataloging-in-Publication Data
Fickling, Meera.
 NAFTA and climate change / Meera Fickling and Jeffrey J. Schott.
    p. cm.
 Includes bibliographical references and index.
 ISBN 978-0-88132-436-5
 1. Free trade—Environmental aspects—North America. 2. Free trade—Government policy—North America. 3. Greenhouse gas mitigation—Economic aspects—North America.
 4. Environmental policy—North America. 5. Climatic changes—Government policy—North America. I. Schott, Jeffrey J., 1949- II. Title.
 HF1746.F53 2011
 363.738'746097—dc23
                          2011028494

Contents

Tables

Figures

Preface

For the past two decades, Institute research has informed the public debate on the North American Free Trade Agreement (NAFTA). Gary Hufbauer and Jeffrey Schott's 1992 book, *North American Free Trade: Issues and Recommendations,* examined the economic benefits and challenges of deepening North American economic integration. Their follow-up volume, *NAFTA: An Assessment* (1993), provided the first independent analysis of NAFTA and was widely cited during the ratification process in all three countries. Subsequent Institute studies have assessed the economic impact of NAFTA on North American trade, investment, labor, and the environment, including most notably Hufbauer et al.'s *NAFTA and the Environment: Seven Years Later* (2000) and Hufbauer and Schott's *NAFTA Revisited: Achievements and Challenges* (2005).

NAFTA and Climate Change builds on this body of research and is part of a broader series of studies on the intersection of climate change policy and trade undertaken by the Institute with the generous support from the Doris Duke Charitable Foundation. In 2008, we published Trevor Houser et al.'s *Leveling the Carbon Playing Field*, which analyzed the potential impact of US efforts to reduce greenhouse gas (GHG) emissions on carbon-intensive US manufacturing and assessed how to maintain an equal footing for carbon-intensive industries as trading partners move at different speeds and adopt a variety of policies to reduce emissions. Gary Hufbauer, Steve Charnovitz, and Jisun Kim's *Global Warming and the World Trading System* (2009) further evaluated whether proposed US climate change legislation complied with WTO rules and suggested a way for the WTO to provide policy space for countries to reduce emissions and maintain competitiveness while preserving an open trading system.

NAFTA and Climate Change was originally intended to complement these studies by examining the effect of national climate change policies on North American economic integration. Climate change legislation introduced in the US Congress in 2009 presaged a new "cap-and-trade" regime that would gradually reduce overall emissions of GHGs while easing the adjustment burdens on US industries and consumers through a mix of subsidies and trade measures. Little attention had been focused, however, on how US climate legislation could affect trade and investment in North America—even though the Waxman-Markey bill that passed the House of Representatives in summer 2009 contained an "international reserve allowance program" that would essentially function as a tariff against carbon-intensive goods imported from countries that did not implement climate change legislation as strong as that of the United States. The implications for our NAFTA partners, Canada and Mexico, were unclear.

The Senate failed to pass a climate change bill in 2010, and the new Republican majority in the House of Representatives after the 2010 mid-term election effectively froze new national legislation for the near future. Despite the dim prospects for comprehensive federal legislation, however, climate policies have continued to advance at the state and provincial level. Though these actions will have much more modest GHG impacts, state and provincial laws still have important effects on North American trade and investment.

This book offers the first comparative analysis of these national and subnational policies and their implications for North American integration. The authors, Meera Fickling and Jeffrey Schott, conclude that a coordinated North American approach to climate change policy can contribute importantly to the achievement of each country's GHG mitigation goals in a way that reduces frictions among different policies and minimizes adverse economic impacts. To that end, they offer recommendations in the final chapter on how NAFTA initiatives could support environmental initiatives and establish notable precedents for broader regional and global climate change efforts to sharply reduce GHG emissions.

During the course of the project, the authors benefited significantly from collaborative research with sister institutions in Canada and Mexico, especially the C. D. Howe Institute in Toronto, CEDAN in Mexico City, and Canada's National Roundtable for the Environment and the Economy. These groups provided both substantive guidance on climate change policies in their countries and forums for discussion of our initial analyses and policy recommendations. We also appreciate the efforts of the secretariat of the NAFTA Commission for Environmental Cooperation (CEC), which facilitated our research and gave us the opportunity to present our findings to the annual meetings of the Joint Public Advisory Committee and NAFTA's environmental ministers.

The Peter G. Peterson Institute for International Economics is a private, nonprofit institution for the study and discussion of international economic policy. Its purpose is to analyze important issues in that area and to develop and communicate practical new approaches for dealing with them. The Institute is completely nonpartisan.

The Institute is funded by a highly diversified group of philanthropic foundations, private corporations, and interested individuals. About 35 percent of the Institute's resources in our latest fiscal year was provided by contributors outside the United States. The Doris Duke Charitable Foundation, Cargill Inc., Caterpillar Inc., Chevron Corporation, and GE Foundation provided generous support for this study.

The Institute's Board of Directors bears overall responsibilities for the Institute and gives general guidance and approval to its research program, including the identification of topics that are likely to become important over the medium run (one to three years) and that should be addressed by the Institute. The director, working closely with the staff and outside Advisory Committee, is responsible for the development of particular projects and makes the final decision to publish an individual study.

The Institute hopes that its studies and other activities will contribute to building a stronger foundation for international economic policy around the world. We invite readers of these publications to let us know how they think we can best accomplish this objective.

C. FRED BERGSTEN
Director
August 2011

Acknowledgments

This book benefited immensely from the advice and constructive comments of a number of experts in Canada, Mexico, and the United States, including Keiko Alvarez, Dale Beugin, Wendy Dobson, Jennifer Haverkamp, Evan Lloyd, David McLaughlin, Antonio Ortiz-Mena, Alejandro Posadas, and Luis Rubio. We also thank our Peterson Institute colleagues William Cline, Trevor Houser, and Gary Hufbauer, who read the entire manuscript and provided extensive comments and constructive critiques.

Special thanks are due to Isabel Studer of the Center for Dialogue and Analysis in Mexico City, who has established a network of North American organizations engaging in research on climate change policy cooperation. Her conferences and workshops provided a valuable forum for discussing early drafts of our work and helped enrich our understanding of both Mexican policies and the broader environmental issues in North America. Similarly, we are grateful to David McLaughlin and his colleagues at the National Roundtable on the Environment and the Economy in Ottawa for sharing their ongoing work with us and offering insightful commentary on our manuscript.

Finally, we appreciate the generous support of the Doris Duke Charitable Foundation and extend our deep gratitude to Madona Devasahayam, Susann Luetjen, and Edward Tureen of the Peterson Institute publications department for the many hours they spent producing this book.

1

Introduction

The North American Free Trade Agreement (NAFTA) entered into force on January 1, 1994, just as the international community was warming to the task of reducing greenhouse gas (GHG) emissions in order to counter the adverse effects of climate change. The United States, Canada, and Mexico participated under United Nations auspices in the drafting of the Kyoto Protocol, which committed developed countries to begin lowering their aggregate emissions and to help developing countries formulate and finance GHG mitigation strategies. Canada and Mexico ratified the Kyoto Protocol; US officials signed the protocol but never submitted the treaty to Congress for ratification.

Addressing climate change and the need to sharply reduce GHGs represents a big challenge for the NAFTA partners. North America is home to less than 7 percent of the world's population but is responsible for almost a quarter of global emissions of carbon dioxide, the most important GHG.[1] The United States accounts for the vast majority of North American, and almost 19 percent of global, GHG emissions (see table 1.1). As a consequence, the climate policies adopted by the United States will substantially impact both its NAFTA partners and prospects for a new global climate regime.

From the start, the NAFTA partners recognized the need to confront climate change problems and reduce national emissions. In October 1995, the environmental ministers of the three countries declared their intent to cooperate on climate change issues, encouraging inter alia diffusion of GHG mitigation technologies, restoration and enhancement of carbon sinks, and exchange of data and research (CEC 1995). The NAFTA partners commissioned several

---

1. World Resources Institute, Climate Access Indicators Tool, http://cait.wri.org (accessed on September 17, 2010).

Table 1.1 Greenhouse gas emissions, 1990 and 2006 (CO_2 equivalent)

Country/grouping	1990 Million metric tons	1990 Metric tons per capita	1990 Tons per million dollars of GDP	2006 Million metric tons	2006 Metric tons per capita	2006 Tons per million dollars of GDP	1990–2006 Change in total emissions (percent)
United States	6,127	24.5	867	7,060	23.6	617	15
Canada	592	21.3	1,089	718	22.0	850	21
Mexico	507	6.1	1,227	709	6.8	1,061	40
NAFTA	7,145	19.8	891	8,413	19.3	649	18
China[a]	3,823	3.4	8,598	7,551	5.8	3,956	98
India[a]	1,388	1.6	5,130	2,215	2.0	3,437	60
Brazil[a]	576	3.9	1,149	862	4.6	1,167	50
Japan	1,269	10.3	306	1,337	10.5	263	5
World[a]	30,055	5.7	1,238	37,767	5.8	983	26

	1990	2006
US/NAFTA (percent)	86	84
US/world (percent)	20	19
NAFTA/world (percent)	24	22

a. 2006 data not available; 2005 data used instead.

Note: The column "tons per million dollars of GDP" measures GDP in constant 2000 US dollars.

Sources: UNFCCC (UN Framework Convention on Climate Change); GHG Data, www.unfccc.int (accessed on June 10, 2011), Semarnat (Secretariat of Environment and Natural Resources), Statistical Database, www.semarnat.gob.mx (accessed on June 7, 2011); World Bank, *World Development Indicators,* http://data.worldbank.org/data-catalog/world-development-indicators (accessed on June 10, 2011).

climate change studies in the mid-1990s, but the initial work of the NAFTA Commission for Environmental Cooperation (CEC) was sidetracked for much of the next decade, as US support cooled after the US Congress failed to ratify the Kyoto Protocol. In the interim, the levels of GHG emissions rose significantly throughout North America; none of the three countries reduced its overall levels of GHG emissions despite notable declines in emissions intensity (CO_2 equivalent emissions per unit of output). As shown in table 1.1, US GHG emissions rose by 15 percent between 1990 and 2006. Canada's performance was even worse, a 21 percent increase over 1990 levels. Mexico's emissions, though still low on a per capita basis, increased by 40 percent during the same period.

Meanwhile, global emissions increased by 26 percent, compared with 18 percent in the NAFTA region. The task of mitigating global warming has become more difficult and costly over time, and dealing with climate change will require substantial changes not only by the NAFTA partners but also by other major emitting countries.

While the NAFTA record to date on climate change has not been stellar, there have been some encouraging recent developments. After years of neglect, the NAFTA partners have begun to pursue policies at the state, provincial, and national levels to mitigate GHG emissions and to encourage consumers and producers to adapt to less carbon-intensive sources of energy. To date, most of these actions have been taken in a piecemeal manner by various states and provinces, and have involved the imposition of new limits on emissions and standards for the production and use of clean energy.

Broader climate policies, however, face uncertain prospects. Although the outlook for US climate legislation looked fairly rosy after the House of Representatives passed the Waxman-Markey climate bill in June 2009, efforts subsequently stalled in the Senate. Since then, federal actions have focused primarily on regulations covering auto emissions and fuel economy standards, while efforts to craft legislation implementing cap-and-trade or other broader schemes to reduce GHGs have faced substantial roadblocks. With Congress at an impasse over climate change policies, the US Environmental Protection Agency (EPA) has begun to formulate regulations under existing statutory authorities that would require large electric power generation plants and carbon-intensive industries to achieve modest emissions reductions over the medium term.

Climate initiatives will continue to face a chilly reception in Congress, and US inaction will retard progress in Canada and Mexico as well. Canadian policymakers worry that their own energy-intensive industries, most of which trade heavily with the United States, could be placed at a competitive disadvantage if new carbon tax and regulatory policies raise the cost of doing business in Canada compared with the United States. Meanwhile, Mexican commitments made at the 2009 UN climate change conference in Copenhagen and elsewhere were conditioned upon substantial financial assistance from developed countries. This expectation may well be unrealistic, as Mexico has a relatively high income compared with other countries that have also asked for climate-related aid. The lack of a US cap-and-trade regime further reduces the likelihood that the United States will set aside substantial funds for climate change finance in Mexico.

The most likely scenario, in the short term, is scattershot implementation of state and provincial climate change programs, combined with modest doses of federal regulation. Although state environmental leadership in the past has proven invaluable as a laboratory of innovation and has tended to prompt stricter federal standards, the state regulations currently on the table cannot produce anything close to the reductions required to fulfill the commitments made by the United States and Canada in Copenhagen in December 2009.

Moreover, while ad hoc measures to limit GHG emissions are certainly welcome steps, they also create political friction—both within each NAFTA country and between the NAFTA partners—that could generate a backlash against climate policies and raise new barriers to trade and investment in North America. A key problem is the potential for "carbon leakage," or the displacement of carbon emissions from regulated areas to unregulated areas, which raises concerns about the impact of the tax and regulatory burdens on the competitiveness of domestic industries still reeling from the sharp recession of 2008-09. In particular, the threat of leakage provides a disincentive for states or provinces with higher concentrations of carbon-intensive industries—precisely the states that most need to transition to more sustainable methods of producing and consuming energy—to join carbon reduction efforts.

Problems can also arise from incompatibilities among regulatory policies and performance standards adopted by various states and provinces. For example, differing definitions of renewable energy, combined with inadequate networks for transmission and distribution of energy, could hinder economies of scale and make a low-carbon transition more difficult or costly to achieve. Certain state performance standards are designed to favor domestic energy production, raising barriers to trade among states and undermining the eventual goal of reducing emissions.

Substantial regional differences in production and consumption of carbon-intensive energy and goods exacerbate pressures on policymakers to protect carbon-intensive industries, and compensating regions that produce and consume a relatively high portion of energy-intensive goods has become the price of broad-based national support for a climate change mitigation regime. The longer climate change regulation is limited to a small subset of North American jurisdictions, the sharper these differences will become. If this trend continues, it will likely lead politicians to take actions to level the playing field, via subsidies or other measures aimed at offsetting the compliance costs associated with climate policies. Such countervailing actions, however, could have the opposite effect. Adverse knock-on effects on trade and investment in the NAFTA region could risk unraveling the decades-old integration of the North American economies. For that reason, US, Canadian, and Mexican officials need to accord climate change issues higher priority on the NAFTA agenda, even as they formulate their own national climate change policies.

Can the NAFTA partners work together to advance their own national and international climate change objectives? The following section sets out a necessarily brief review of climate change initiatives in the NAFTA region over the past 15 years. To date, the NAFTA record is not encouraging, but there is evidence that the issue is gaining traction in national and regional policy debates.

The NAFTA Experience with Climate Change Issues

The three NAFTA countries have experienced five-year cycles of interest and disinterest in addressing climate change, though few concrete steps were taken even during periods when climate change was discussed. The NAFTA experience can be divided into three periods: early interest (1995–2000); not-so-benign neglect (2000–2005); and refocused attention going forward (2005–2010).

Although environmental agreements have been in place in North America for more than a century, NAFTA launched a new era of trilateral environmental cooperation. The North American Agreement on Environmental Cooperation (NAAEC) was negotiated in 1993—after NAFTA was formally signed but prior to its ratification by national legislatures—primarily to address US concerns about Mexican policies and specific problems in the US-Mexico border region.[2] While Mexican environmental laws were similar to US statutes, they were not well enforced, and US constituencies feared that NAFTA would encourage footloose US firms to relocate south of the border to take advantage of cheap labor and pollution havens. The NAAEC established a new trilateral institution, the CEC, to encourage cooperative policies among the three NAFTA countries, develop regional projects to address environmental problems, and counter environmental abuses and violations of NAFTA commitments through limited dispute settlement powers. Mexico and Canada reluctantly acceded to the new negotiations, recognizing that the Clinton administration would not pursue ratification of the trade agreement until supplemental pacts on labor and the environment were appended to the core treaty text. The environmental side pact helped overcome congressional opposition to the NAFTA implementing legislation, which passed the House of Representatives by a narrow margin in November 1993.

Climate change issues were discussed in the CEC during NAFTA's first five years, but the topic soon drifted off the trilateral agenda as the US political debate soured on the new United Nations climate treaty. Canada and the United States signed the Kyoto Protocol. However, the US signature was not definitive; in July 1997, the Byrd-Hagel Resolution passed the Senate by a vote of 95 to 0, clearly signaling that Congress would not ratify the treaty unless it required developing countries to reduce or limit emissions—which, as negotiated, it did not. Neither the Bill Clinton nor the George W. Bush administra-

---

2. For a summary of NAAEC provisions, see Hufbauer et al. (2000, chapter 3).

tion submitted the treaty for ratification, and President Bush subsequently withdrew the United States from the protocol in 2001. Although Canada did ratify the Kyoto Protocol, it was not until 2000 that it released its Federal Action Plan, which aimed to reduce GHGs by 65 million metric tons (mmt) between 2008 and 2012 and thus achieve about one-third of Canada's Kyoto target. It committed C$500 million to a list of measures to reduce emissions, but this spending did not successfully slow the growth in Canada's GHG emissions. Subsequent plans were likewise unsuccessful, and proposals to enact a cap-and-trade system for large emitters were never implemented.

Unlike the United States and Canada, Mexico was not required to commit to GHG reductions in the Kyoto Protocol, yet its efforts in this area were comparable to those of its NAFTA neighbors. In the 1990s, Mexican climate initiatives focused primarily on developing basic information on the nature of national emissions problems. In 1992, the National Autonomous University of Mexico and the National Institute of Ecology—the research branch of Mexico's Secretariat of Environment and Natural Resources (Semarnat)—established the National Scientific Program on Global Climate Change to coordinate research and develop core data. Mexico published its first greenhouse gas inventory in 1995. Like the United States and Canada, however, Mexican officials talked about climate change but did not translate intentions into effective action. Mexico's emissions intensity spiked in 1997 before falling back to previous levels in 1999 and essentially leveling off over the past decade. Mexico's GHG intensity is now about 25 percent greater than the Canadian level and about 70 percent greater than the US level (see figure 1.1).[3]

Guided by its constituent members, the CEC discussed climate change but took little concrete action—not surprising since the CEC was from the outset burdened by a large agenda with a small budget. Although CEC ministers resolved in 1995 to "facilitate cooperation on issues of mutual interest in the areas of climate change" and directed the CEC Secretariat to do so (CEC 1995), these initiatives were put into deep freeze after the harsh US congressional reaction to the Kyoto Protocol cited above. Nevertheless, the CEC has published a yearly Pollutant Release and Transfer Registry report on industrial emissions, which provides a factual foundation for future cooperation on GHG emissions in North America.

By contrast, another new North American institution, the North American Development Bank (NADB), contributed little to efforts to reduce GHGs. Part of this poor performance was due to the NADB's initial narrow focus; it was created to garner political support in Congress for NAFTA ratification by

3. See UNFCCC (UN Framework Convention on Climate Change), GHG Data, www.unfccc. int (accessed on June 10, 2011); Semarnat (Secretariat of Environment and Natural Resources), Statistical Database, www.semarnat.gob.mx (accessed on June 7, 2011); and World Bank, *World Development Indicators*, http://data.worldbank.org (accessed on June 10, 2011). These intensities were calculated using GDP expressed in constant 2000 US dollars. If calculated using purchasing power parity GDP, Mexico's GHG intensity is actually lower than that of the United States and Canada.

Figure 1.1   Greenhouse gas intensity in the United States, Canada, and Mexico, 1990–2008 (emissions per million dollars of GDP at constant 2000 US dollars)

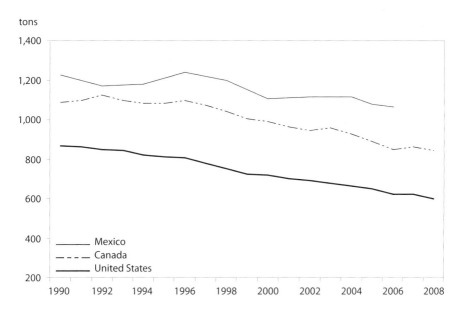

tons

Note: Data for Mexico are available only up to 2006.

Sources: UNFCCC (UN Framework Convention on Climate Change), GHG Data, www.unfccc.int/ (accessed on June 10, 2011); Semarnat (Secretariat of Environment and Natural Resources), Statistical Database, www.semarnat.gob.mx (accessed on June 7, 2011); World Bank, *World Development Indicators*, 2010, http://data.worldbank.org/data-catalog/world-development-indicators (accessed on June 10, 2011).

targeting funding for wastewater treatment plants in the US-Mexican border region. The NADB also was inhibited by limited funding, unwieldy lending requirements, and lack of borrowing capacity in Mexican municipalities.[4] While the NADB has the potential to contribute to climate change initiatives, it was not given the means or direction to do so. We discuss how these failings can be redressed in the final chapter.

The next five-year cycle, through 2005, could be called the era of energy exuberance. The three NAFTA countries gave short shrift to climate change issues. Instead, in the aftermath of the terrorist attacks of September 11, 2001, and the subsequent war in Iraq, concerns about energy security overwhelmed the environmental agenda. Expanding US oil and gas production took precedence over, and diverted attention from, environmental initiatives. Indeed, the Bush administration's chief environmental advocate, EPA administrator Christine Todd Whitman, resigned in frustration over the dismissive approach

---

4. For a fuller discussion of the NADB, see Hufbauer and Schott (2005).

of White House officials to the broad environmental agenda. US GHG emissions increased during this period despite improvements in US energy intensity indices, as shown in figure 1.1.

In Canada, the Alberta oil boom upstaged efforts to comply with Kyoto obligations. Rising oil prices made exploitation of the oil sands economically attractive, and new investment surged into the Fort McMurray area. With booming production in the oil and gas sector, along with rapid growth in road transport, Canadian GHG emissions continued to increase, thus undercutting even the modest goals set out in the 2000 Federal Action Plan.[5]

In Mexico, climate initiatives foundered for several reasons, including the difficulty of reforming energy policy, cutting transport emissions, and curbing deforestation. Oil production began a slow decline, which in turn constrained public funding for environmental projects and enforcement, since the revenues of the state oil monopoly, PEMEX, provide a substantial share of federal government revenues. Facing rapid depletion of one of Mexico's major oil fields, Mexican politicians argued about energy reforms and ended up doing very little. Simply put, President Vicente Fox and his administration were unable to master the art of compromise with a Mexican Congress that was no longer dominated by a single party, and climate change initiatives were among the areas that suffered accordingly.

Since 2006, however, all three countries have begun to refocus attention on climate change policies. A number of factors have contributed to this transition, including a growing international commitment to climate change action in response to the growing weight of scientific evidence reported by UN agencies and academic research—popularized by Al Gore's widely distributed documentary *An Inconvenient Truth*. Polling in the United States showed an increase in public concern about climate change between 2000 and 2008.[6]

In Canada, the federal government in 2007 issued Turning the Corner, a plan for an intensity-based target system for GHG emissions; the plan's implementation, however, has been put on hold, as federal and provincial officials continue to debate the cross-cutting effects of resource policies and climate change initiatives. In 2010, Canada set its pledge to the same target as the United States and promised to follow through only if the United States did. As policy stalled in Ottawa and federal officials awaited signs of how US policy would evolve, individual provinces began to adopt GHG mitigation and adaptation strategies. Several provinces introduced carbon taxes and regulations to reduce GHG emissions, and several established trust funds to finance research and development of carbon sequestration technologies. In some cases, prov-

---

5. The oil and gas industry was the second-largest contributor to the rise in greenhouse gas emissions between 2000 and 2008; the largest was road transportation. See Environment Canada (2010).

6. Public concern about climate change has decreased markedly since 2008, however, due inter alia to the economic downturn in late 2008 and 2009, which shifted priorities to restoring output and employment growth.

inces set out emissions intensity limits and renewable electricity requirements for electric utilities in order to encourage cleaner technologies. Ontario set the goal of phasing out coal-fired electricity generation. These initiatives are discussed in more detail in chapter 3.

In Mexico, the Calderón government commissioned the consulting firm McKinsey and Company, and other experts to develop a long-term strategy for reducing GHG emissions (Centro Mario Molina 2008). In light of that analysis, Mexico pledged in December 2008 to reduce emissions 50 percent below 2002 levels by 2050, an aggressive target for a developing country. It further committed in December 2009 to reduce emissions 51 mmt below business-as-usual levels by 2012, equivalent to a 6.4 percent cut, and 30 percent below business-as-usual levels by 2020. Its 2009 Special Climate Change Program (PECC) outlines a roadmap to meet these goals. We discuss this plan and the challenges to its implementation in chapter 4.

The most notable, albeit incomplete, developments in climate change policies have taken place in the United States since the start of the Obama administration in January 2009. At that time, the US Congress began deliberations on a comprehensive climate change bill that would create a cap-and-trade system for reducing GHG emissions over time. The American Clean Energy and Security Act passed the House of Representatives in June 2009. The bill included a number of provisions aimed at building broad-based political support for a new carbon regime, including free allowances to major emitters and emissions offset provisions that help mitigate compliance costs. The bill set the goal of reducing total US emissions by 20 percent from 2005 levels in 2020; its cap-and-trade component required covered sources to reduce emissions 3 percent by 2012, 17 percent by 2020, and 83 percent by 2050. However, parallel legislation in the US Senate failed to advance in 2009–10. Absent federal legislation, US policy will continue to be formulated and implemented by the laws and regulations of individual states and by EPA regulation pursuant to the Clean Air Act of 1970. The next chapter discusses the US regulatory initiatives in more detail.

While national cap-and-trade schemes have foundered, nascent carbon trading regimes are under construction in three major North American regional initiatives: the Regional Greenhouse Gas Initiative (RGGI), the Midwest Greenhouse Gas Accord (Midwest Accord), and the Western Climate Initiative (WCI). Of the three, the WCI and the RGGI are more advanced, and the RGGI is the only framework that is currently being implemented; see table 1.2 for a comparison of the WCI and RGGI.

The members of the RGGI include Connecticut, Delaware, Maine, Maryland, Massachusetts, New Hampshire, New Jersey, New York, Rhode Island, and Vermont. The program covers only electric power generators. The cap-and-trade system is designed to stabilize emissions from 2009 to 2014 and reduce emissions 10 percent below 2009 levels by 2018.

The WCI is an agreement among California, Montana, New Mexico, Oregon, Washington, British Columbia, Manitoba, Québec, and Ontario to reduce emissions 15 percent below 2005 levels by 2020. Members accounted

Table 1.2   Regional Greenhouse Gas Initiative (RGGI) versus Western Climate Initiative (WCI)

	RGGI	WCI
Target	Emissions 10 percent below 2009 levels by 2018.	Emissions 15 percent below 2005 levels by 2020.
Time frame	Emissions stabilized from 2009 to 2014; 2.5 percent decline in emissions per year from 2015 to 2018, for a total of 10 percent decline by 2018.	Emissions from electrical generators, large industrial and commercial combustion, and large industrial process emissions capped starting in 2012. Residential emissions and emissions from small industrial/commercial combustion and transportation fuel combustion capped starting in 2015.
Regulated entities	Electric power generators are regulated; imported electricity is not regulated.	Regulation is as close to the point of emission as possible, or where fuels "enter commerce in the WCI partner jurisdictions."
Offsets	Offsets must come from within the RGGI region.	Offsets must come from within North America.

Sources: RGGI (2008); WCI (2010).

for 10 percent of US emissions in 2005 and 50 percent of Canadian emissions in 2008.[7] Unlike the RGGI, the WCI envisions an economy-wide cap by 2015. California has led US states on implementation, publishing a draft regulation under Assembly Bill 32 in 2009. With the exception of California, however, the US member states appear unlikely to muster the political will to overcome the serious resistance to cap-and-trade that has recently emerged in the United States.

While GHG regulation has proceeded unevenly in the United States and Canada at the federal and subnational levels, the issue has gained increasing salience on the NAFTA agenda. As we discuss below, the North American Leaders' Summit in August 2009 refocused attention on the importance of climate change issues and instructed officials to develop a trilateral working plan for consideration at their next summit. At the CEC ministerial meeting in August 2010, North American environmental ministers also committed to improving the comparability of data gathering and inventories for mitigation and adaptation projects (CEC 2010). Whether the NAFTA partners can then turn the plan into concrete actions is another story. To do so, each country will have to sidestep the politically sensitive concerns about the impact on production and employment that have so far confounded efforts to formulate national policies.

---

7. Data are from US state environmental agencies and Environment Canada and can be found in Fickling (2010).

Implications for NAFTA of Climate Change Policies

Why has it been so hard to begin to reduce GHG emissions in North America? Part of the answer lies in the heavy dependency on fossil fuels and part in the failure to adequately attribute the environmental costs of carbon emissions to the producers and users of those fuels. As a result, industries and individuals have pursued investments or purchases based on a "free carbon" development model—leading to more coal-fired electricity generation plants, more gas-guzzling vehicles, and more suburban housing and strip malls in place of farms and forests.

Reducing GHGs will require changes in the way firms and individuals produce and consume, whether by improving the efficiency of energy use, by mandating the use of cleaner energy, by changing the vehicles that people drive, or simply by imposing a price on carbon emissions. Still reeling from the sharp recession of 2008–09, NAFTA policymakers face enormous pressure to achieve this economic shift without hurting consumers or damaging the competitiveness of local industries—that's why draft US legislation in 2009 contained generous offsets and subsidies for at least a decade to buffer emitters and consumers alike from the higher costs that would arise from pricing carbon.

Unfortunately, some of the ways in which politicians react to this pressure could have adverse impacts. Some measures to compensate consumers and industries could dampen incentives to adapt and conserve or could provide a de facto subsidy for certain domestic producers. Some measures would erect trade barriers to protect domestic industries, a practice that probably runs afoul of international rules. As a consequence, the measures could have unintended consequences for economic welfare and foreign relations that spill over into the NAFTA region.

NAFTA officials face three major challenges in crafting climate policies. First, they need to manage the regional impacts of climate laws and regulations, which could vary significantly depending on a region's sources of electricity generation, its economic activities, and its natural resource endowments. Second, they need to address ongoing competitiveness concerns, i.e., the implications of climate policies for production and employment, and trade and investment, in the NAFTA region. Third, they need to upgrade and better align their energy and transport infrastructure to improve energy efficiency and expand use of renewable energy sources and low-carbon fuels, which could at least partly alleviate regional competitiveness pressures. The following subsections describe each of these challenges.

Managing Regional Differences

Production and use of energy and energy-intensive goods differ widely both between the NAFTA partners and within each country. Producers of fossil fuel–based energy such as coal and petroleum will be vulnerable to climate change policies almost by definition—emissions reductions will require a reduction in the burning of fossil fuels. Producers of energy-intensive goods such as aluminum, steel, paper, cement, and chemicals will be vulnerable if they cannot switch to low-carbon energy sources, make energy-efficiency improvements, or pass along extra costs to consumers. Moreover, many producers of energy-intensive goods are located in areas served by high-carbon energy. The concentration of fossil fuel extraction and energy-intensive manufacturing in certain regions amplifies concerns about industrial competitiveness.

Legislative politics is the art of appeasing local constituencies, and the politics of climate change has been no exception. In crafting climate change legislation, political leaders have favored measures that reflect regional resource endowments and the interests of important industries in their area. What constitutes good politics, however, may not constitute effective policy to mitigate GHG emissions. Below, we provide an overview of the regional breakdown of the sources of energy and emissions in each country, and we describe some of the frictions among local, national, and continental interests that could result from climate policy. These issues will be discussed further in the following chapters.

United States

Despite periodic calls for "energy independence," the United States is a net importer of oil and gas from its North American neighbors and other countries, and it is likely to remain so in the future. This dependence on foreign sources of energy could cause significant tension between the need to reduce greenhouse gas emissions and the need to ensure a steady supply of energy from nations that support US security interests.[8] The only major fossil fuel that is not imported is coal, which the United States uses heavily for electricity. Coal-fired electricity generation accounts for about half of US consumption—and is the most carbon-intensive fuel for electricity production.

Across the country, regional differences in total GHG emissions embedded in overall consumption are relatively small. However, the differences among GHG emissions embedded specifically in electricity consumption are larger. In general, midwestern and southeastern states are more likely to obtain electricity from fossil fuel–based sources, whereas Pacific and northeastern states are more likely to obtain electricity from less carbon-intensive sources.[9]

Industries that use a large amount of energy account for a greater percentage of GDP and employment in the southeastern United States and certain midwestern states—the same areas that tend to have the most carbon-intensive

---

8. A prominent recent example of this conflict is the construction of the Keystone XL pipeline from Canada to the US Gulf Coast. Despite concerns raised by the EPA regarding additional GHG emissions from the oil sands, the State Department (which is required to certify the pipeline) seems to favor the project. See chapters 2 and 3 for a more detailed discussion.

9. All energy consumption statistics are from the Energy Information Administration, 2010, Net Generation by State by Type of Producer by Energy Source (EIA-906).

sources of energy.[10] Fossil fuel production is also concentrated in these areas. Not surprisingly, congressional representatives from the Midwest and the South tend to take a pessimistic view of the effect of carbon pricing on their states' economies and have demanded that legislation favor their states' vulnerable industries as a condition of their support.

These regional disparities are likely to be exacerbated by differences in state GHG regulations; the state regulation patchwork is expected to remain the dominant climate policy paradigm in the short term. States with the most robust climate change policies tend to be those that already emit relatively fewer GHGs per capita, and they are overwhelmingly concentrated in the Northeast, West, and Great Lakes area, with the Northeast and the West Coast states leading the pack. As these states reduce emissions, states in the Southeast and Midwest are continuing along a fossil fuel–intensive growth path—and they may thus increasingly resist climate change policies that raise their energy costs and put their industries and workers at a competitive disadvantage.

Canada

Canada is the only NAFTA country that currently gets a large share of its electricity from a zero-carbon source. Hydropower provides almost 60 percent of Canada's electricity.[11] Yet, with growing oil sands production, it will be a challenge to reduce total Canadian GHG emissions over the coming decade.

In Canada, managing regional differences means balancing competing provincial interests: the pursuit of climate change objectives versus the exploitation of natural resources. In the East, the provinces of New Brunswick, Québec, and Ontario have relatively large manufacturing sectors. Even the most fossil fuel–dependent of these three provinces, New Brunswick, derives 40 percent of its electricity from zero-carbon sources. In the West, energy-intensive manufacturing is dominated by British Columbia and Alberta. British Columbia derives over 90 percent of its electricity from hydropower. Alberta, however, derives three-quarters of its electricity from coal and has a large energy-intensive manufacturing presence.[12]

Alberta largely owes its economic boom to oil sands production. A recent report by the National Roundtable on the Environment and the Economy estimates that Alberta would lose a great deal of economic growth from the oil sands if climate policy were implemented (NRTEE 2011). As a result, Alberta has sharply different priorities with regard to mitigating GHG emissions than eastern provinces. And although the Saskatchewan oil sands are at an earlier stage of development than Alberta's, the conventional oil and gas industry is a major player in Saskatchewan as well.

---

10. This subject is discussed in more detail in chapter 2.

11. Statistics Canada (2009, table 2).

12. Ibid.

The concentration of carbon-intensive activities in Alberta and Saskatchewan creates a substantial division of interests between these western Canadian provinces, which rely on petroleum exports for economic growth, and the eastern Canadian provinces, which are home to a substantial manufacturing sector. All energy-intensive Canadian exports stand to lose from a failure to harmonize climate change regulations with those of countries abroad; if Canada's regulations are mismatched with—either more or less stringent than—those of major export markets such as the United States, the European Union, and Japan, there is a threat of lost competitiveness. However, Alberta and Saskatchewan also stand to lose a great deal from regulation of the carbon embedded in petroleum extraction, and petroleum firms and politicians in these provinces have advocated that Canadian regulations minimize compliance costs for the petroleum industry or at the very least take steps to compensate the western provinces for the additional costs.[13] If the petroleum sector is held to a more lenient standard than other industries, it will force the manufacturing, residential, and transport sectors to achieve greater emissions reductions in order to meet Canada's mitigation goals—a disadvantage to the eastern Canadian provinces, which do not earn substantial revenues from oil production.

Mexico

In contrast to its northern neighbors, Mexico's top priority is to cut greenhouse gas emissions from transportation, which make up the largest part (34 percent) of its sectoral emissions portfolio. Mexico also relies heavily on fossil fuels, albeit cleaner ones than the United States, obtaining 55 percent of its energy from petroleum and 32 percent from natural gas.[14] The government's most recent GHG emissions reduction plan, the PECC, envisions reduced methane emissions from production of hydrocarbons and wastewater treatment plants. In addition, Mexico has long struggled with deforestation, and reduced emissions from deforestation and degradation (REDD) plays a central role in the PECC.

While Mexico has set aggressive goals compared to other developing countries, meeting these goals will require it to overcome considerable capacity and financial constraints. Mexico would benefit from bilateral technical and financial assistance from its NAFTA partners, as well as the development of an integrated North American climate regime that would enable environmentally sound Mexican projects to sell carbon credits to the other two countries.

---

13. For example, Premier Brad Wall of Saskatchewan advocated strongly against a federal policy that failed to give credit for provincial investment in carbon capture and sequestration. See Brad Wall, speech given at the Canadian Energy Forum held by the Energy Council of Canada, Ramada Hotel Ballroom, Regina, Saskatchewan, February 9, 2010.

14. Energy Information Administration, International Energy Statistics, 2010.

Mexico ranks fourth in the world in terms of number of registered certified emissions reductions.[15]

Addressing Competitiveness Concerns

Climate change policies can have substantial implications for both the level and distribution of production and employment, as well as for prospective decisions on new investments within the North American region. Depending on the stringency of the policies regulating the use and price of carbon, lowering GHG emissions could affect what goods are produced as well as where and how they are produced. That's why the issue has been accorded high priority on the agenda of the North American Leaders' Summit.

As noted above, some standards may cause carbon leakage, simply displacing GHG-producing activities to unregulated jurisdictions without preventing the resultant environmental harm. Much of the attention has been focused on carbon leakage at the producer level—the movement of carbon-intensive production from places where carbon-intensive production is expensive to places where carbon-intensive production is cheap. Certain highly traded, energy-intensive sectors have expressed concern about this possibility, and as a result the issue of leakage has become a major focus of attention in the debate over cap-and-trade programs. The potential for producers to move out of regulated jurisdictions has become a significant issue at the state level as well as the federal level, due to the patchwork nature of state policies; officials from several states have expressed concern about leakage as a result of their participation in the Western Climate Initiative.

State performance standards such as low-carbon fuel standards (LCFS) and renewable portfolio standards generally regulate at the point of consumption.[16] For this reason, interstate leakage would primarily consist of movement of carbon-intensive consumption from places where carbon-intensive consumption is expensive to places where carbon-intensive consumption is cheap. For example, a utility selling electricity sourced from both renewable and coal-fired electricity to several states could, in theory, respond to a renewable portfolio standard by shifting its sales so that all of its renewable offerings went to the regulated state and its coal-fired offerings went to the unregulated state. We discuss this possibility in later chapters.

These concerns about leakage are speculative; models produce mixed results as to whether climate change policies will cause substantial relocation in the near term (Houser et al. 2008). Nevertheless, concerns regarding competitiveness of regulated producers have become central to the political rhetoric surrounding legislation. In response, politicians have vetted a mixture

---

15. UN Framework Convention on Climate Change, Registered Projects by Host Party, http://cdm.unfccc.int/Statistics/index.html (accessed on June 8, 2011).

16. The exception is the renewable portfolio standard, which regulates producers.

of subsidies, exemptions, and border measures to compensate local industries. Border adjustments are popular as a means of leveling the playing field, especially because they do not incur budgetary costs. These so-called competitiveness measures could potentially trigger countervailing measures from affected jurisdictions. Such reactions would increase the costs of, and possibly provoke a public backlash against, environmental measures enacted to reduce greenhouse gas emissions.

Particularly in the US Congress, border adjustments have been a prerequisite for passage of any cap-and-trade bill and undoubtedly will resurface when climate legislation is vetted in the future. Although Canada's cleaner electricity generation portfolio makes most of its industries less likely to experience these border measures (Dachis 2009), Canada still faces the risk of US protectionism if it does not adopt a climate policy similar to that of its southern neighbor (NRTEE 2009). Border measures are also a concern for Mexico, which is unlikely to adopt comparable emissions-reduction policies in the near term.

Canadian officials, meanwhile, worry that a failure to coordinate climate policy with the United States could jeopardize Canada's energy-intensive manufacturing exports. If the energy and regulatory costs of Canadian policy are substantially higher than those in the United States, investments in new production plants could be diverted from Canadian to US sites. Gary Hufbauer and Jisun Kim (2009) note that a few industries have a high volume of intra-industry trade, suggesting that they have a high degree of firm-to-firm competition across the border. Marginal changes such as the imposition of border measures would be likely to render firms in these industries less competitive than their counterparts in the other country. As the industries identified by Hufbauer and Kim (2009) account for up to 11 percent of Canadian manufacturing employment in certain provinces, Canada has a strong interest in aligning its climate policies (including energy use standards) with those in the United States in a way that promotes mitigation and adaptation and reduces the risk that Canadian production will relocate in response to a GHG "pollution haven" south of its border.

Canada's concerns about US policy are not limited to federal legislation. The government of Stephen Harper also wants to encourage development of Alberta's oil sands resources, and it has been concerned about foreign regulations that could curtail oil sands exports if widely adopted. California's low carbon fuel standard is one such regulation. The LCFS requires retailers of transport fuels to reduce the GHG emissions intensity of their products by 10 percent from 2006 levels by 2020. Toward this end, the LCFS regulation assigns GHG intensity values to different fuels; because oil sands crude receives a separate life-cycle analysis from "conventional" fuels, its GHG intensity value is likely to be substantially higher. The Canadian government has expressed its concern that the LCFS is discriminatory, as it favors domestic production over Canadian oil sands exports. We discuss this issue further in chapter 2.

Aligning Infrastructure and Policy

Compounding the competitiveness problem is the fact that energy infrastructure and distribution networks are not fully integrated in the NAFTA region. In particular, distribution networks for low-carbon energy need to be improved. Continent-wide infrastructure and streamlined policies could lower costs and stimulate trade in low-carbon goods.

The North American countries need to develop new cross-border infrastructure as part of a serious effort to reduce emissions. Transmission will need to be updated across the continent; given the high level of interconnection between the United States and Canada, it will be essential to coordinate the construction of a "smart," 21st century grid. Meanwhile, the US market could drive development of Mexico's abundant wind, solar, and geothermal resources, if the limited transmission capacity between the two countries is substantially upgraded.

Some progress has already been made on this front. Manitoba and Saskatchewan are in the preliminary stages of spearheading a Western Energy Corridor for renewable and nonrenewable transmission, and New Brunswick and Maine have proposed to build a Northeastern Energy Corridor to transmit renewable energy between the two jurisdictions.[17] However, much work remains, particularly in terms of US-Mexico transmission networks.

Creation of a favorable environment for innovation requires coordination not only of infrastructure but also of the policy framework within which businesses must operate. Harmonization of standards would allow businesses to operate in a more predictable and uniform regulatory environment and create economies of scale that could encourage innovation and reduce compliance costs. A predictable regulatory environment and economies of scale could in turn alleviate competitiveness impacts resulting from the regulations. To be sure, policymakers require the freedom to tailor policies to local conditions, and local jurisdictions often serve as laboratories of innovation, where policies are tested and proven before being implemented at higher levels of government. However, there is ample room to coordinate regulation without taking away the benefits of localization. Opportunities to do so can be found in renewable standards, where coordinated definitions of renewable energy could promote investment, and cap-and-trade systems, which might be linked through mutual acceptance of other jurisdictions' carbon allowances.

Common North American Interests

Despite the challenges, the three NAFTA partners have mutual interests in a coordinated and comprehensive energy strategy. First, they share a common environment and a long history of bilateral cooperation on environmental

---

17. Government of New Brunswick, New Brunswick and Maine Support International Energy Corridor, press release, March 25, 2009, www.gnb.ca (accessed on June 9, 2011).

problems. The United States and Canada have signed acid rain and other trans-boundary pollution agreements; the earliest US-Mexico treaty that established the precedent to the current International Boundary and Water Commission dates back to 1889. More recently, the North American Development Bank has provided funding and coordination for environmental infrastructure in the US-Mexico border region.

Second, a large share of the energy consumed in North America is produced in North America, and a lot of it is traded across the US-Canada and US-Mexico borders. How energy is produced, used, and traded has a large impact on GHG emissions and affects how each country can adapt to a low-carbon future.

The NAFTA region has an interdependent but not fully integrated energy market. Canada is the leading source of US oil imports (about 20 percent of total US crude oil imports came from Canada in 2010, and about 70 percent of the crude oil produced in Canada was shipped to the United States); Mexico consistently ranks second or third. Combined, Canada and Mexico accounted for about 35 percent of US oil imports in 2010.[18] In 2010, this energy trade was running at an annual rate of almost $50 billion between the United States and Canada and at almost $30 billion between the United States and Mexico.[19]

Natural gas is the second-largest component of NAFTA energy trade. Canada is almost solely responsible for bridging the gap between natural gas production and natural gas demand in the United States, providing 90 percent of US imports, or about 16 percent of consumption. US-Canada natural gas trade totaled about $31 billion in 2008. Likewise, the United States provides about half of Mexico's natural gas imports, or 14 percent of its consumption. Natural gas trade between the United States and Mexico totaled $694 million in 2008.[20]

US-Canada electricity trade is also notable. While Canadian imports do not make up a large portion of most US states' electricity portfolios, they comprise a major percentage of total consumption in a few border states. Vermont obtains almost 40 percent of the electricity consumed from Québec, and North Dakota and Minnesota obtain more than 10 percent of electricity consumed from Manitoba. US exports are less significant to Canadian provincial electricity supply; the exception is British Columbia, which gets almost 10 percent of its electricity supply from American states. While Mexico lacks sufficient electricity interconnections with the United States (only Baja California and California are connected), its wind and solar resources are a potentially significant source of electricity for both the Mexican and US markets.

---

18. Energy Information Administration, US Crude Oil Imports by Country of Origin, http://eia.doe.gov (accessed on June 14, 2011).

19. US International Trade Commission Dataweb, www.usitc.gov.

20. Energy Information Administration, Summary of US Natural Gas Imports, 2007–2008, available at http://eia.doe.gov (accessed on July 9, 2011).

In addition, the North American countries share a common interest in minimizing distortions for North American trade and investment. As noted above, US congressional draftsmen have included border adjustments in virtually all climate change legislation. While such provisions seem aimed at China and other Asian countries, they actually could have a more significant impact on trade from Canada and Mexico. Canada is the largest supplier by far of energy-intensive manufactures to the United States, including steel (20 percent of US imports), cement (53 percent of US imports), paper (52 percent of US imports), and aluminum (55 percent of US imports). Canadian exports of these four products, plus chemicals, totaled $17 billion in 2009.[21] As a result, both countries are justifiably concerned about maintaining a level North American playing field for energy-intensive manufacturing. Decisions that affect energy production or consumption in one country will have significant spillover effects throughout the region.

In addition to minimizing adverse competitiveness impacts within North America, North American energy-related firms need to stay ahead of global competition. As the Canadian Council of Chief Executives (2010) points out, China has become a world leader in global green technology investment, and South Korea has announced that it will invest 1 percent of GDP in clean technology over five years. Arguing that "long-term energy innovation will be fundamental to enhancing Canada's global brand" (Canadian Council of Chief Executives 2010, 48), the council has pleaded for an integrated North American energy and environmental strategy to spur this investment. Industry support for such policies has not been as widespread in the United States, but key voices have echoed the council's call. In a January 2011 op-ed, the CEO of General Electric called clean energy one of the "areas where America can lead."[22] In a speech that cited increasing competition for energy resources from countries such as China, Exxon CEO Rex Tillerson called in 2009 for a revenue-neutral carbon tax.[23] Various firms, including PG&E, Duke Energy, Dow Chemical, and Caterpillar, endorsed an economy-wide price on carbon in 2009 (USCAP 2009). Mexico's oil company, PEMEX, has also tried to move ahead of the global cap-and-trade curve with an internal initiative to achieve modest emissions reductions.

Finally, North American countries all require a livable climate—and thus share an interest in reinforcing global climate negotiations. Climate change mitigation remains a global collective action problem. North America emits only a fifth of the world's greenhouse gas emissions—and the rest of the world's emissions are growing far faster than North America's. Whereas North

---

21. Ibid.

22. Jeffrey Immelt, "A Blueprint for Keeping America Competitive," *Washington Post*, January 21, 2011.

23. Rex Tillerson, Strengthening Global Energy Security, speech at the Woodrow Wilson Center, Washington, DC, January 8, 2009.

American emissions on the whole increased by 17 percent between 1990 and 2005, total world emissions increased 26 percent.[24] These data clearly show that North America alone cannot mitigate climate change.

Near-term prospects for a fully comprehensive global accord are not bright. In the absence of a binding global agreement, regional cooperation on climate change issues assumes greater importance and could eventually help pave the way for stronger multilateral cooperation. Indeed, the text negotiated at the 16th Conference of the Parties (COP-16) meeting of the UN Framework Convention on Climate Change (UNFCCC) in Cancún in December 2010 calls for bilateral and regional cooperation on climate financing and REDD to supplement the financial provisions negotiated within the UNFCCC. North America is one of the most important regions of the world in climate terms, containing as it does 3 of the top 15 greenhouse gas emitters in the world—including the second-largest emitter, the United States.[25] These countries have already begun to play an active role in international negotiations. Mexico spearheaded a "green fund" proposal for international climate financing during the run-up to the 2009 Copenhagen talks, and it hosted the sequel to the Copenhagen session in Cancún in late 2010. US negotiators, meanwhile, offered $100 billion in climate finance from developed countries in return for commitments to climate action from key developing countries.

As a consequence, cooperation on climate change within the North American region could set a meaningful precedent for North-South cooperation globally. To the extent that North American cooperation can serve as a model for the multilateral stage, it could have benefits that extend much farther than North American emissions alone.

Plan of the Book

This book assesses both the challenges facing the three NAFTA partners in reducing GHG emissions and the implications of climate initiatives in each country for North American economic integration. In separate chapters, we examine climate change policies in the United States, Canada, and Mexico, and then assess what needs to be done to coordinate or integrate state, provincial, and national climate programs both bilaterally and regionally. While climate change laws and regulations pose the risk of new frictions in North American trade and investment, they also create incentives for cooperation through new bilateral and regional initiatives. The study therefore concludes with recommendations on how the three countries can better use NAFTA to advance their national environmental objectives.

---

24. World Resources Institute, Climate Access Indicators Tool, 2010, http://cait.wri.org.

25. Ibid.

2

United States

Due to the size of its economy, its importance as an energy consumer, and the quantity of its greenhouse gas (GHG) emissions, the United States has the lead role in setting climate policy in North America. In the United States, climate policy is formulated at both the federal and state levels and implemented through tax and regulatory policies. The key existing federal authorities under which GHGs can be regulated are the Clean Air Act of 1970 and transport rules such as the corporate average fuel economy (CAFE) standard established by the Energy Policy Conservation Act of 1975. Currently, state and federal policies are applied on a piecemeal basis. Recent attempts to put together a comprehensive federal climate policy fell apart in 2010 when the Senate failed to act on legislation comparable to the American Clean Energy and Security Act (ACESA) that passed the House of Representatives in June 2009. A comprehensive carbon-pricing approach was deferred indefinitely.

As a consequence, US climate policy today consists of a patchwork of state climate laws and regulations combined with federal regulation seeking to set limits on utility, automobile, appliance, and other sectoral emissions. Crafting a coherent climate policy in such an awkward legal environment is a difficult task, and one made all the more challenging due to regulatory uncertainty. Environmental Protection Agency (EPA) rules face challenges in the courts and in Congress; some states that had previously committed to joining regional cap-and-trade systems, such as Arizona, Utah, and Montana, have since either pulled out formally or indicated that they will not go through with their commitments; and funding for state and federal regulatory initiatives may not be forthcoming. State and local governments thus cannot know what the future regulatory picture will be, further complicating the coordination problem. States are skittish about adopting climate policies without comparable action by other states, as they are concerned about losing competitiveness if they go it alone. As states citing these reservations back away from climate legislation, they encourage other states to follow suit.

The purpose of this chapter is to assess the rapidly slowing pace of US climate initiatives and outline some of the reasons why it has evolved as it has. Efforts at top-down policy development—based on broad congressional legislation like ACESA—have given way to bottom-up efforts by US states and federal regulators, recalling the era of not-so-benign neglect of federal climate policy of a decade ago. For that reason, we first turn to the differences among states that complicate climate policy formation. Divergent state energy sources and industrial concentrations contribute to the fear that climate policy will disproportionately impact certain states' economies. This fear makes it more difficult to obtain a consensus on federal legislation, and it discourages state legislators from joining nascent state climate efforts.

Next, we describe major state and federal legislation and evaluate the programs' trade impacts and the risk of leakage they present. We assess the responses that state and federal governments have developed to address this risk. We also point out features of state legislative initiatives that could be made more compatible with each other and with Canadian and Mexican initiatives. This discussion will set the stage for subsequent chapters on Canadian and Mexican policies, as well as for our recommendations in the concluding chapter.

Distribution of GHG Emissions

The consequences of climate change policy for various regions have received a great deal of attention in state and federal legislatures. For legislators, concerns regarding the regional distribution of the costs of climate change policy fall into two broad categories. The first is differences in the embedded GHG consumption of the average person within a state or region. Numerous federal and state politicians have pointed out the high consumption of coal-fired electricity in various jurisdictions. A scathing 2009 *Wall Street Journal* op-ed, referencing the high level of per capita emissions in interior states such as Wyoming and North Dakota, accused cap-and-trade of facilitating a massive wealth transfer from the interior United States to the lower-carbon coastal states.[1]

Rhetoric aside, the actual distribution of GHG emissions presents a more nuanced picture. In terms of total economy-wide emissions, regional differences in consumption are relatively small. Analyzing a national cap-and-trade program, Kevin Hassett, Aparna Mathur, and Gilbert Metcalf (2008) find a maximum variation in household burden between regions of 0.4 percent of household income. Likewise, Dallas Burtraw, Richard Sweeney, and Margaret Walls (2008) find a relatively small overall divergence across regions in US CO_2 intensity of total consumption; this finding suggests that the effects of climate

---

1. "Who Pays for Cap and Trade?" *Wall Street Journal*, March 9, 2009, A18.

policies on the average consumer would probably vary relatively little from state to state.

The one area where GHG content varies widely among states is electricity generation. Burtraw, Sweeney, and Walls (2008) find that household emissions from electricity range from nearly zero tons per capita in California and Nevada to approximately 6 tons per capita in the Ohio Valley. Thus, a tax or regulatory policy focusing specifically on electricity would have more diverse impacts on regions.[2]

Regional disparities in generation to date do not necessarily indicate that renewable potential does not exist in areas such as the Southeast and Midwest, which have historically obtained more energy from fossil fuels. Researchers at the World Resources Institute estimate that, using available technologies, the Southeast can derive more than 30 percent of its electricity needs from renewable resources, at no more than the cost of the most expensive conventional power (Creech et al. 2009). However, developing cleaner sources of electricity will involve substantial infrastructure investments and policy improvements in states that have a history of coal-fired power production.

The second category of concerns about the regional distribution of the costs of climate change policy regards the relative GHG intensity of key industries within each state or region—and the effect of climate regulation on jobs within these industries. While total employment effects of climate policy are not expected to be large, effects in specific industries are likely to be significant. Warwick McKibben and Peter Wilcoxen (2009) find that nationwide emissions targets consistent with the United States' Copenhagen commitments would cause employment in the coal mining and crude oil and gas industries to decline by much more than in any other industry. Effects in electricity production and petroleum refining also become significant in 2025. Other industries, however, are barely affected. Mun Ho, Richard Morgenstern, and Jhih-Shyang Shih (2008) model the effects of a $10 per ton carbon tax and find relatively small employment effects in all but the coal mining sector in the short run. In the medium and long run, petroleum refining, gas production, and coal mining lose 4 to 10 percent of workers. This study assumes full overall employment in the medium and long run.

Table 2.1 reports state-by-state employment in the coal, oil, and gas sectors, and table 2.2 does the same for energy-intensive, trade-exposed industries (EITEs). Coal mining in the United States largely takes place in Wyoming and the southern Appalachian states, particularly West Virginia and Kentucky. Pennsylvania and Virginia also have a large number of workers employed in coal mining, and although coal does not account for an especially large portion of their overall state economies, it is locally important in certain areas of both states. Oil and gas extraction is a huge industry for Wyoming, employing

---

2. These diverse impacts contribute to the intense debate on the EPA climate change regulations.

Table 2.1   Employment in fossil fuel industries, selected states

Rank	State	Total employed in coal production[a]	Total employed in oil and gas production[b]	Percent of total workers in coal production	Percent of total workers in oil and gas production	Percent of total workers in fossil fuel industry
1	Wyoming	6,883	22,374	2.5	8.1	10.6
2	Louisiana	185	65,535	0.0	3.5	3.5
3	West Virginia	19,582	6,205	2.6	0.8	3.4
4	Oklahoma	235	51,715	0.0	3.4	3.4
5	Alaska	70	9,323	0.0	3.0	3.0
6	New Mexico	2,163	16,991	0.3	2.0	2.3
7	Texas	2,542	219,971	0.0	2.2	2.2
8	North Dakota	1,062	4,678	0.3	1.3	1.6
9	Montana	1,159	4,819	0.3	1.1	1.4
10	Kentucky	16,755	3,034	0.9	0.2	1.1
41	Florida	0	614	0.0	0.0	0.0
42	Massachusetts	0	198	0.0	0.0	0.0
43	Rhode Island	0	30	0.0	0.0	0.0
44	New Hampshire	10	20	0.0	0.0	0.0
45	Oregon	0	70	0.0	0.0	0.0

46	South Carolina	0	74	0.0	0.0	0.0
47	North Carolina	20	38	0.0	0.0	0.0
48	Iowa	0	20	0.0	0.0	0.0
49	District of Columbia	0	0	0.0	0.0	0.0
50	Vermont	0	0	0.0	0.0	0.0
	United States	84,832	537,956	0.1	0.4	0.5

a. North American Industry Classification System (NAICS) codes 2121 and 213113.
b. NAICS codes 211, 213111, 213112, and 324110.

Note: In cases where the census provides a range of values for a data point, we used the midpoint in our calculation of total employment.

Table 2.2 Employment in energy-intensive, trade-exposed industries (EITEs), selected states

Rank	State	Number of employees in EITEs (thousands)	Total nonfarm employment (millions)	Percent of employment in EITEs
1	West Virginia	14.17	0.76	1.9
2	Tennessee	41.36	2.78	1.5
3	Louisiana	26.6	1.85	1.4
4	South Carolina	25.01	1.91	1.3
5	Alabama	24.97	1.98	1.3
6	Maine	6.68	0.61	1.1
7	Kentucky	19.56	1.85	1.1
8	Indiana	31.34	2.97	1.1
9	Ohio	50.77	5.44	0.9
10	Arkansas	11.05	1.199	0.9
11	Pennsylvania	45.48	5.76	0.8
12	Wisconsin	22.11	2.87	0.8
13	Wyoming	1.84	0.28	0.7
14	Texas	65.46	10.07	0.7
15	Oklahoma	9.52	1.54	0.6
36	New York	20.09	8.62	0.2
37	South Dakota	0.89	0.40	0.2
38	Colorado	4.94	2.28	0.2
39	Maryland	5.53	2.59	0.2
40	Connecticut	3.57	1.68	0.2
41	Massachusetts	6.42	3.25	0.2
42	North Dakota	0.69	0.35	0.2
43	California	27.54	15.06	0.2
44	Rhode Island	0.88	0.49	0.2
45	New Mexico	1.28	0.83	0.2
46	Florida	9.58	8.00	0.1
47	Arizona	3.00	2.63	0.1
48	Nevada	1.23	1.28	0.1
49	Alaska	0.18	0.32	0.1
50	Hawaii	0.00	0.62	0.0

Notes: Totals are calculated using industries presumptively included in the rebate program under the American Clean Energy and Security Act of 2009. In cases where the census provides a range of values for a data point, we used the midpoint in our calculation of total employment.

Source: US Census Bureau (2007).

8 percent of the state's workers.[3] Other large oil and gas states are Texas, Oklahoma, New Mexico, Louisiana, and Alaska. By contrast, the District of Columbia, Vermont, and Iowa have barely any workers employed in the fossil fuel industries.

EITEs do not make up as great a percentage of employment as the extractive industries, but they also tend to be found in greater numbers in certain states (see table 2.2). In terms of absolute numbers of employment, Texas tops the list, with about 65,500 workers, followed by Ohio (50,000), Pennsylvania (45,000), and Tennessee (41,000). In terms of percentage of total employees, West Virginia is the most exposed, with almost 2 percent of its employment in EITEs. Other states derive more than 1 percent of employment from EITEs, including Tennessee, South Carolina, Maine, Louisiana, Kentucky, Indiana, and Alabama, but in general EITEs do not constitute a large portion of overall state economies.

These disparities in the GHG intensity of states' key industries affect state and federal policy differently. Federal policy must take explicit steps to equalize the effects on different regions, whether by compensating states with relatively high GHG emissions through free allowances or cash payments, or through other means such as payments to lower-income and middle-income families.[4] Meanwhile, state tax and regulatory policies are contained systems; revenue collected from regulated entities is recycled back to state citizens, not spread evenly over fifty states. Thus, state regulations do not require regulatory gymnastics to smooth out the regional effects of climate policy on households.

However, state climate taxes and regulations are more susceptible to carbon leakage than federal regulations. US states are more highly integrated than most countries, making it easier for firms to move to unregulated states. Firms shifting within country do not face the cultural, informational, and institutional barriers faced by firms moving overseas—it is easier to shift operations from Sacramento to Houston than from Sacramento to Beijing. Moreover, states cannot easily implement border measures to stem carbon leakage without running afoul of constitutional constraints on the regulation of interstate commerce.

As a result, the presence of coal-fired electricity or energy-intensive industries in a state can be a powerful incentive not to adopt climate policy in the first place. The thirty states that have adopted renewable portfolio standards tend to be located in areas that consume electricity that is less GHG-intensive to begin with. The states slated to adopt cap-and-trade policies by 2012—California plus the Northeast members of the Regional Greenhouse Gas Initiative (RGGI)—also lead the pack in terms of low household GHG output and low GHG intensity of electricity production. Statewide cap-and-trade programs in these states

---

3. Though climate policy would reduce employment in the oil industry, it would boost employment in the natural gas industry, which would be expected to replace coal in the short term.

4. Burtraw, Sweeney, and Walls (2008) point out that the regions most affected by climate policy also tend to be lower-income on average.

will likely incur higher overall costs because, in contrast to high-carbon states, low-carbon states have already implemented many of the negative-cost and low-cost "low-hanging fruit" policies and production methods available to them, and thus additional emissions reductions will be more expensive.[5] However, not surprisingly, these states have comparably small political constituencies built around carbon-intensive, trade-exposed manufacturing and energy industries.

This tendency of "clean" states to adopt climate legislation and "dirty" states to eschew climate legislation could have one of two effects. On the pessimistic side, it could have a cascading effect. As states fall further behind leaders such as California in reducing emissions, they will be less likely to acquiesce to stringent federal regulations, because the benefits from such legislation will be perceived to go to the early actors. On the other hand, an optimistic outlook is that early state action by a few states could provide a model for other states to follow. The more states that join a regional cap-and-trade system, the lower the risk of carbon leakage—and the more attractive cap-and-trade will be to additional states and to federal legislators.

State Initiatives

In this section, we describe the state initiatives on the table and assess their implications for North American integration. Until 2009, US initiatives to address greenhouse gas emissions were largely formulated at the state level in areas such as renewable electricity standards, GHG performance standards for electricity, energy-efficiency resource standards, automobile GHG standards, and low-carbon fuel standards (LCFS). California has been at the forefront, implementing auto emissions and other performance standards that have exceeded federal clean air mandates and regulating areas where federal policies have not been developed. California's leadership on the environment has been codified in the 1970 Clean Air Act, which allows California and only California to set air pollution standards that exceed federal standards; other states may adopt either the California or the federal standards. Though there are notable differences among policies at the subfederal level, California policies are emulated by a number of states (and Canadian provinces).

In the absence of federal legislation, individual states are taking the lead in advancing climate policy in the United States. States are developing and implementing several programs that establish, inter alia, caps on industry and transportation emissions, renewable portfolio standards, and low-carbon fuel standards. If lawmakers are able to put into action all of the state initiatives currently on the table, coverage of these programs will be extended to the greater part of the United States.

---

5. Under a national GHG reduction scheme, low-carbon states could get credit for their early action and thus come out ahead of high-carbon states. However, this type of credit is not possible in state cap-and-trade systems.

States have provided important political momentum toward a broader climate change strategy. State policies serve as a laboratory of innovation, wherein policies can be tested and refined on a small scale before they are implemented on a national level. Such laboratories have led to the inclusion of a renewable portfolio standard, first implemented by Iowa and later adopted by thirty states, in proposed national climate change legislation. Stricter state automobile emissions standards have galvanized federal regulators to adopt similar measures.

States also tailor regulations to local conditions. Building codes and local utilities are traditionally regulated by states, and in the areas of electricity and energy efficiency, regulatory failures often occur at the state and local levels. Recognizing that states might be better equipped to address these facets of climate policy, ACESA delegated the implementation of specific energy and building programs to the states.

Because state standards are implemented on a smaller scale, they are sometimes able to bypass political influences that would deter similar federal measures. Historical first movers on the environment have been able to gather political momentum behind cap-and-trade bills and performance standards much more quickly than is possible at the national level.

However, state and local standards, if not coordinated, can present significant disadvantages. As noted in the introductory chapter, there are three main challenges to implementing successful climate change legislation: smoothing over regional differences in energy endowments, addressing carbon leakage, and better aligning state, regional, and federal regulations.

The issue of carbon leakage has received a great deal of attention in US debates over federal and state climate policies. Because state standards regulate a much smaller area than national standards, they are even more susceptible to leakage (Wiener 2007). With regard to state standards, leakage can occur in two ways. First, carbon-intensive production can move from places where it is expensive to places where it is cheap. Second, state regulation of consumption may lower the price of carbon-intensive goods such as electricity and transport fuel, making it more attractive to consume them elsewhere. In relatively fungible markets, trans-state firms have the option of selling their lowest-carbon offerings (for example, renewable electricity or fuels) within regulated jurisdictions and selling their higher-carbon offerings (for example, coal-fired electricity or oil sands products) to unregulated jurisdictions, without changing their overall production patterns. Standards such as California's LCFS regulate at the point of consumption and would be susceptible to this kind of leakage.

A patchwork of varying state standards can also send a confusing signal to markets, lessening incentives for companies to innovate. Firms may be uncertain whether state and provincial standards will eventually be rendered irrelevant by federal preemption, and they may have difficulty adapting national or international product lines to local standards. Lack of coordination can also prevent states from capturing efficiencies from comparative advantage and economies of scale, thus increasing costs.

The challenge will be to prevent leakage and appease pressures on locally important industries without making policies insular by closing off markets for energy and energy-intensive goods. To meet this challenge, local and federal governments will need to coordinate standards as best they can, and in this way build synergies among different policies and manage competitiveness impacts.

Below, we analyze the implications of some of the most prominent and widely adopted types of state standards for trade flows and carbon leakage. These standards include economy-wide carbon reduction programs, renewable portfolio standards, and the low-carbon fuel standard.

Economy-Wide Carbon Reductions

Overview of Policies

The Regional Greenhouse Gas Initiative is the only multistate cap-and-trade system with mandatory emissions caps currently in force in the United States. Members include Connecticut, Delaware, Maine, Maryland, Massachusetts, New Hampshire, New Jersey, New York, Rhode Island, and Vermont. As explained in Chapter 1, the program initially covers only electric power generators—about 95 percent of the electricity sector falls under the cap-and-trade regime—but coverage may expand later to other sectors such as transportation. The goal of the cap-and-trade system is to stabilize emissions from 2009 to 2014 and reduce emissions by 2.5 percent per year between 2015 and 2018, for a total decline in emissions of 10 percent by 2018.

The program requires one-quarter of a state's allowances to be auctioned, and 5 out of 10 states have decided to auction all allowances. According to the RGGI overview, revenue from auctions will be used to fund incentives for end-use efficiency, lowering the cost of the program to the consumer, although it is up to individual states exactly how this revenue will be allocated. Offset allowances are permitted for 3.3 percent of compliance obligation. In the case of price spikes, this percentage might be increased. Early reduction allowances were provided for reductions made between 2006 and 2008. Through March 2011, the RGGI conducted 11 auctions. Allowance prices have so far been low, averaging $2.45 per ton of emissions, and have declined significantly since the start of the program.[6] Emissions reductions have not yet commenced, however; prices could rise in 2015, as emissions limits are lowered.

The Western Climate Initiative (WCI) is an agreement among Arizona, California, Montana, New Mexico, Oregon, Utah, Washington, British Columbia, Manitoba, Québec, and Ontario to reduce emissions 15 percent below 2005 levels by 2020. California has led in developing an economy-wide cap-and-trade program, publishing a draft regulation under Assembly Bill 32 in 2009. Starting in 2012, the program will cover electrical generators distributing within the

---

6. Regional Greenhouse Gas Initiative, Auction Results, www.rggi.org/co2-auctions/results (accessed on May 10, 2011).

WCI region (including emissions imported from non-WCI jurisdictions), large industrial and commercial combustion, and large industrial process emissions. Residential emissions, small industrial and commercial combustion, and transportation fuel combustion will be regulated starting in 2015. In general, regulation is as close to the point of emission as possible, with the exception of fuels for small-scale combustion, where regulation is upstream. The WCI has been designed to accommodate linkages to other regions as well.

Although the 11 states and provinces listed above initially joined the WCI, their participation has since dwindled. All US states except California have either officially or unofficially suspended plans to implement cap-and-trade. Of the Canadian member provinces, only Québec remains firm in its commitment to start on time (as of June 2011). British Columbia has indicated that it may be able to begin on time, but it is revisiting its cap-and-trade plans in light of booming natural gas development.[7] Ontario and Manitoba have indicated that they will join after the program starts, though Ontario's plans have been put on hold until the October 2011 provincial elections. A Conservative victory in the fall would render implementation of WCI commitments highly unlikely, while the current Liberal premier has indicated he remains committed to cap-and-trade.

California has already formulated its proposed regulations to comply with the WCI, and its targets, sectoral coverage, and start dates mirror those of the WCI. Its program covers 85 percent of total state GHG emissions; in addition, sectors that are not required to reduce their GHG emissions under the new law may voluntarily opt in to the cap-and-trade system. California's regulation of GHGs from transport fuels and electricity, like that of the WCI as a whole, is at the point of entry into the state; that is, generators, producers, and importers of energy are all held responsible for the carbon embedded in their products. While about half of allowances are auctioned, 42 percent are given away free of charge to electrical distribution utilities and trade-exposed manufacturing industries.

As of June 2011, the start date of California's cap-and-trade program remained uncertain due to a court ruling in favor of advocates from a collection of NGOs, the Association of Irritated Residents, that requires the state to examine alternative policies for reducing GHG emissions. The San Francisco Superior Court ordered the California Air Resources Board (CARB) to halt plans for the cap-and-trade program until it had complied with this requirement, although an appeals court then temporarily allowed the state to move ahead with rulemaking.[8] Depending on how this court battle plays out, implementation of California's cap-and-trade system could be delayed, although the program is still expected to move forward eventually.[9]

7. Shawn McCarthy, "B.C., Ontario Hinder California Green Plan," *Globe and Mail*, April 13, 2011.

8. PointCarbon, "California Poised to Overcome Carbon Market Lawsuit," *Carbon Market North America*, June 17, 2011.

9. Jonathan Bardelline, "California Cap-and-Trade May Start a Year Behind Schedule," *GreenBiz*, June 3, 2011, www.greenbiz.com/ (accessed on June 10, 2011).

Implications for North American Integration

If federal legislation fails to regain traction, the patchwork of state regulation currently in place will define North American climate policy in the near future. Point Carbon (2010) estimates that a scaled-down WCI—with California, New Mexico, Oregon, Washington, and the four Canadian provinces—plus a revamped RGGI would cover approximately 485 companies, reducing US and Canadian 2020 emissions by 107 million metric tons (mmt) and 83 mmt respectively, or about a 2 percent reduction from 2005 levels in the United States and an 11 percent reduction from 2005 levels in Canada.

As with other patchwork state standards, there is potential for carbon leakage. The amount of carbon leakage that occurs through these cap-and-trade programs will depend on the sectors regulated, the point at which they are regulated, and the ease of reshuffling production relative to the ease of actual emissions reductions. The RGGI regulates electricity producers at the point of production; this obligates power plants within the RGGI region to reduce emissions but does not regulate electricity imported into the RGGI region. Electricity distributors are thus able to simply import "dirty" electricity to replace local production without actually reducing the GHG emissions of electricity consumed within the RGGI region (Bushnell, Peterman, and Wolfram 2007). Modeling projections for the RGGI described in the RGGI Leakage Working Group report estimate emissions leakage of 18 to 27 percent of net GHG emissions reductions through 2015, resulting from the siting of new power plants outside the RGGI region (RGGI Emissions Leakage Multi-State Staff Working Group 2007).[10] The report qualifies these results by pointing out that the model does not take into account location-specific demand, access to transmission, local siting and permitting considerations, or the ability to obtain a power purchase contract with a local distributor. In addition, all of the RGGI states have adopted stringent renewable portfolio standards that should produce emissions reductions from power plants over the RGGI time frame, creating an additional regulatory incentive to change the way power is generated within the area.

Also mitigating potential emissions leakage are transmission and generation constraints of neighboring states, as well as long-term contracts with power plants within the RGGI jurisdiction. The cap-and-trade program is predicted to cause only small electricity price increases—3 to 4 percent—by 2018 (Gittell and Magnusson 2008).[11] Given that state-to-state price variation

---

10. Although subsequent evaluations have been conducted since the start of the program in 2008, they have not estimated leakage. Substantial leakage pressures likely have not existed to date, as allowance prices have remained very low and emissions levels have remained substantially under the RGGI cap. See Jackson Morris, comments submitted to the RGGI stakeholder meeting on behalf of the Pace Energy and Climate Center, September 13, 2010, www.rggi.org (accessed on May 16, 2011).

11. See also Regional Greenhouse Gas Initiative at www.rggi.org (accessed on May 25, 2011).

is already much larger (table 2.3), it seems unlikely that such price increases would create strong incentives to import power from outside the jurisdiction. The cost of transmission between states alone is estimated to exceed the extra cost imposed by cap-and-trade (RGGI Emissions Leakage Multi-State Staff Working Group 2007). For these reasons, leakage will probably be quite a bit more modest than modeled.

The final reason why leakage from the RGGI will be limited is because the economic recession of 2009 sharply lowered the region's emissions trajectory below business as usual, even through 2020 and beyond.[12] Because the number of emissions permits allocated by RGGI was determined before the recession hit, it was set far too high. As a result, emissions are less likely to "leak" to outside areas because they were reduced through forces outside the RGGI program. If energy usage were to rebound faster than predicted, leakage could be a concern.

The WCI, by contrast, regulates the first jurisdictional deliverer. In other words, imports of electricity and fuel are regulated at the point where they enter the WCI jurisdiction, and domestic power plants and industrial facilities are regulated at the point of emission. This approach prevents firms from simply importing fossil fuel–fired electricity in order to escape regulation. In theory, jurisdictions could swap electricity distribution; WCI local electricity distributors could import clean electricity from other jurisdictions, and other jurisdictions could import dirty electricity from the WCI. Such a strategy would require clean electricity to be available outside the WCI jurisdiction, however, and given that the major Canadian producers of hydropower accessible to western US states are included in the WCI region, the availability of sufficient clean electricity outside the WCI jurisdiction is not nearly enough to meet the WCI cap.[13] Additionally, importation of clean electricity from outside the WCI jurisdiction is subject to significant transmission costs and other barriers.

There could, however, be some leakage in terms of the location of carbon-intensive industries. Assuming the use of carbon offsets, the caps envisioned by the WCI are expected to increase electricity prices by 6.6 percent and oil prices by 6.5 percent for industry (WCI 2008). Unlike the RGGI, the WCI has not done any official modeling of expected leakage due to these effects, although a 6.6 percent increase in electricity prices would not significantly increase costs for any energy-intensive industry except perhaps primary aluminum.[14] Several outside researchers have conducted studies of leakage within

---

12. Bill Dornobos, "The RGGI Emissions Cap: Is It Too Forgiving?" Yale Center for Environmental Law and Policy, April 1, 2011, http://environment.yale.edu/envirocenter (accessed on June 10, 2011).

13. Energy Information Administration, Retail Sales of Electricity by State by Sector by Provider, www.eia.doe.gov (accessed on May 16, 2011).

14. The cost of primary aluminum production would increase by 1.3 percent. Other industries' costs would increase by less than 1 percent. These numbers are calculated using data found in Ho, Morgenstern, and Shih (2008).

Table 2.3   Cost caps and maximum effective retail rate increases under state renewable portfolio standards

State	Maximum effective retail rate increase	February 2009 average existing retail rates (cents per kilowatt hours)	Average maximum increase (cents per kilowatt hours)	Industry maximum increase (cents per kilowatt hours)
Arizona	To be determined	8.65	n.a.	n.a.
California	Cap for portion of cost	12.45	n.a.	n.a.
Colorado	1.6%	7.80	0.12	0.09
Connecticut	6.5%	17.55	1.14	0.92
Delaware	16.3%	12.06	1.97	1.58
District of Columbia	2.5%	13.68	0.34	0.25
Hawaii	0%	20.54	0	0
Iowa	No explicit cap	6.99	n.a.	n.a.
Illinois	1.4%	9.34	0.13	0.11
Massachusetts	3.3%	16.05	0.53	0.46
Maryland	2.1%	13.45	0.28	0.23
Maine	4.8%	14.47	0.69	0.58
Minnesota	No explicit cap	8.00	n.a.	n.a.
Montana	0.1%	7.26	0.01	0.01
North Carolina	1.9%	8.53	0.16	0.10
Nevada	No explicit cap	9.56	n.a.	n.a.
New Hampshire	8.3%	15.50	1.29	1.15

New Jersey	10.6%	14.45	1.53	1.30
New Mexico	1.8%	8.41	0.15	0.11
New York	0.9%	15.27	0.14	0.10
Oregon	4.0%	7.70	0.31	0.19
Pennsylvania	No explicit cap	9.64	n.a.	n.a.
Rhode Island	6.4%	16.20	1.04	0.92
Texas	2.1%	10.73	0.23	0.16
Washington	4.0%	6.98	0.28	0.21
Wisconsin	No explicit cap	9.49	n.a.	n.a.
Utah	Firms are expected to meet standard if "cost effective"	6.26	n.a.	n.a.

n.a. = not applicable

Sources: Energy Information Administration, Retail Sales of Electricity by State by Sector by Provider, www.eia.doe.gov (accessed on March 15, 2009); Wiser and Barbose (2008).

California's cap-and-trade program. Adam Rose, Dan Wei, and Fynnwin Prager (2010) do not find significant leakage potential as a result of California's Assembly Bill 32, although a small amount of leakage could occur in glass and glass product manufacturing, petroleum refining, and miscellaneous mining. On the other hand, David Roland-Holst (2010) finds that a significant percentage of predicted output decline in agriculture, construction, printing and publishing, electrical appliances, and ground transport is made up for by increased imports. The output decline itself does not exceed 1 percent in any of these sectors, however.

The design of the California cap-and-trade system reflects concerns regarding industrial competitiveness. Although the CARB considered imposing adjustments at the border similar to those envisioned by federal legislation, this proposal was rejected due to conflicts with the commerce clause of the US Constitution and potential conflicts with World Trade Organization (WTO) rules (CARB 2010b). Instead, the regulation gives away allowances free of charge on a product-output basis to vulnerable manufacturing industries; 17 percent of the total allowances created are set aside for this purpose (CARB 2010a). The number of allowances given to a firm cannot exceed 110 percent of the maximum annual emissions of a facility between 2000 and 2010.

Richard Morgenstern and Eric Moore (2010) model the effects of free allocations such as those included in California's bill on EITE output and carbon leakage. The authors find that average EITE output losses fall from 1.6 percent to 0.4 percent with free allocations. For the most heavily impacted industry, fertilizers, the output loss falls from 4.7 percent without rebates to 3.2 percent with rebates. This model suggests that output-based allocations could be effective at controlling carbon leakage created by state policies, although states will have to be careful that such allocations are not trade distorting.

The RGGI and the WCI include features that are designed to encourage participation by other states and firms. These features could allay leakage concerns, although in the short run, additional participation is likely to be limited. Both the RGGI and the WCI allow any North American jurisdiction to "observe" their system, enabling states to take an intermediate step before joining. Two former observers, Québec and Ontario, are now members of the WCI.

Even if states choose not to join, the WCI allows North American firms to sell carbon offsets into the system. From a climate standpoint, this is less beneficial than having additional states join. Offsets do not create additional reductions, but simply displace them to other areas. By encouraging outside firms to reduce emissions, however, offset programs can spur low-carbon development outside the region. Such development could potentially mitigate some of the differences among states' carbon intensities of production that currently discourage certain states from supporting climate policy.

Accordingly, offsets may be used toward compliance as part of California's cap-and-trade system. These are limited to 4 percent of each firm's compliance obligation. Total offset credits over the lifetime of the program are limited to

232 million tons CO_2e (CO_2 equivalent). The initial offset protocols that have been established include US forest projects, livestock manure digester projects, urban forest projects, and US ozone-depleting substances projects. The regulation also leaves open the possibility of sector-based offset credits, and offsets for reduced emissions from deforestation and degradation (REDD) will likely be the first sectoral category to emerge.

Renewable Portfolio Standards

The most common local measure implemented in North America, the renewable portfolio standard requires covered utilities to supply a certain percentage of electricity through renewable sources. Over half of US retail electricity sales are covered by a mandatory renewable standard.[15] Although the renewable energy requirement is the most common measure catalogued in our study, measures differ widely across the continent. The most obvious area of divergence is the target percentage of renewable energy to be achieved by a certain date; arguably the least stringent target, in Texas, is 5 percent by 2015, whereas California's target is 33 percent by 2020. (Though Texas nominally has the smallest required percentage of renewable energy, however, the design of its standard has been widely credited with successfully spurring investment in the state.)

In addition, there are many components of the legislation that are less obvious but still crucial to a standard's environmental benefits and industrial effects. One such area is coverage; while legislation in some states covers all utilities, legislation in other states excludes municipal, cooperative, or small utilities. Some states that cover municipal and cooperative utilities adopt a separate, more lenient set of standards for these facilities. Coverage affects the extent to which existing utilities are forced to adopt new sources of generation, which in turn determines the proportion of industries that could suffer higher rates.

Eligibility of resources is another major component of legislation. The level of compatibility between eligible resources and a state's resource concentrations determines the ease with which state utilities can meet a renewable standard—and often, states tailor eligible renewable resources in order to favor in-state industries (Rabe 2006). Sources that are most often eligible to fulfill state renewable energy standards include wind, solar, geothermal, landfill gas, and ocean energy. Often, solar power is prioritized above other renewable energy sources, receiving either a separate requirement or a permit multiplier (e.g., solar generation capacity might be counted 1.2 times as much as other types of renewable generation capacity). Hydropower, biomass, and municipal

---

15. This figure is based on authors' calculations using 2009 data from the Energy Information Administration, Retail Sales of Electricity by State by Sector by Provider, www.eia.doe.gov (accessed on May 16, 2011). Sales are measured in megawatt hours. Some state renewable portfolio standards restrict coverage to certain categories of utilities; due to difficulty finding retail sales data disaggregated by type, this calculation does not take these restrictions into account.

solid waste tend to be given lower priority under a renewable portfolio standard, if such sources are eligible at all. Often, these sources are classified as "second tier," eligible to meet only a limited portion of a renewable requirement. Hydropower is commonly limited to smaller, more environmentally friendly sources or is limited to capacity additions to existing generation facilities. Some states allow energy efficiency to count toward all or part of the target. Several states (e.g., New York and Washington) also include biofuels such as ethanol and biodiesel. Minnesota and Ohio are the only states catalogued that allow coal-fired plants with carbon capture and storage to meet requirements, and Ohio is the only state that permits nuclear energy to meet requirements.[16]

In determining price impacts, one of the most notable features of state renewable standards is the cost cap that most states include, either explicitly or implicitly through mechanisms such as alternative compliance payments. In addition to numeric caps, some states adopt a blanket requirement not to exceed a "reasonable cost"; similarly, Minnesota grades utilities based on "good-faith effort" rather than whether utilities have actually met its standard. Ryan Wiser and Galen Barbose (2008) of the Lawrence Berkeley National Laboratory found that of the states with effective limits on rate increases, only two—Delaware and New Jersey—potentially allow rates to increase by more than 10 percent, and only three—Delaware, New Hampshire, and New Jersey—would allow rates to increase by more than one cent per kilowatt hour (kWh) for industrial customers. Delaware's legislation has the highest allowable price increase, at 16 percent, which would translate into an increase of approximately 1.6 cents per kWh for industrial customers and an increase of approximately 2 cents per kWh for residential customers in the peak target year.[17] These mechanisms limit the extent to which energy costs can rise under a renewable portfolio standard, which in turn limits the standard's effects on industrial competitiveness.

Regional trends emerge both in terms of the proportion of jurisdictions adopting a renewable portfolio standard and in terms of the stringency of the standards adopted.[18] Mandatory renewable standards in the United States are overwhelmingly concentrated in the Pacific Northwest, West, Northeast, and Great Lakes regions. California has adopted the most stringent standard in the United States, requiring all utilities to obtain 33 percent of electricity from renewable sources by 2020. The South and the Plains states largely do not impose mandatory renewable requirements; those that are implemented in these regions (with the exception of the District of Columbia's standard) tend to be weak relative to other states.

---

16. Ohio currently obtains 4.5 percent of energy from nuclear power. See Energy Information Administration, 2010, Net Generation by State by Type of Producer by Energy Source (EIA-906).

17. Figures are calculated using data from Wiser and Barbose (2008) and Ho, Morgenstern, and Shih (2008).

18. For a full listing of key differences, see Fickling (2010).

Implications for North American Integration

Despite the lack of coordination among state renewable portfolio standards, it seems unlikely that the standards will suffer from carbon leakage. Reshuffling electricity distribution to fit the standard should not be a major issue; neighboring states largely do not produce sufficient renewable electricity, so substantial new renewable generation will be needed.[19] It is important to note that there is already a large variation in retail electricity prices among states (see table 2.3). Price variation due to renewable standards is likely to be overwhelmed by this existent variation, especially given that most states' standards cap cost increases below 10 percent.[20]

Cost increases due to the standards are not predicted to be large enough to cause adverse competitiveness effects or affect siting decisions for industrial users of electricity. Researchers at the Lawrence Berkeley National Laboratory compiled a meta-analysis of 28 cost projections for renewable portfolio standards. Most studies project small rate increases, under 1 percent, although two studies predict rate increases above 5 percent (Chen et al. 2007). While these estimates are somewhat questionable due to outdated assumptions,[21] rate impacts have thus far been quite modest and relatively constant, ranging between 0.1 percent and 1.2 percent (Wiser, Barbose, and Holt 2010; Wiser and Barbose 2008).[22] Most renewable policies are still in their ramp-up stage, and impacts could increase as the peak target year approaches. Nevertheless, even if rates increased by the maximum amount allowed under the law for all states with existing cost caps, the cost of producing most electricity-intensive manufacturing goods would increase by less than 1 percent in those states.[23] Prices could increase more in Wisconsin, Pennsylvania, and Nevada, which do not have explicit cost cap mechanisms, but because all three states allow renewable credit trading, it is more likely that their price increases will remain comparable to those in other states.

A greater impediment to North American trade is the barriers that many renewable portfolio standards either directly or indirectly establish for inter-

19. Energy Information Administration, Retail Sales of Electricity by State by Sector by Provider, www.eia.doe.gov (accessed on May 16, 2011); see also Bushnell, Peterman, and Wolfram (2007).

20. Much of this variation existed before most renewable mandates were implemented; for historical data, see Energy Information Administration, Retail Sales of Electricity by State by Sector by Provider, www.eia.doe.gov (accessed on May 16, 2011).

21. The studies tend to significantly underestimate wind prices (which will drive up the price of any renewables program) and natural gas prices (which will drive up the avoided cost of any renewables program). See Chen, Wiser, and Bolinger (2007).

22. Exceptions are Connecticut and Massachusetts. Massachusetts' renewable electricity credit prices have risen significantly since 2002, and Connecticut's have fluctuated. Still, rate impacts of both have remained under 2 percent.

23. This figure is based on authors' calculations using data from Wiser and Barbose (2008) and Ho, Morgenstern, and Shih (2008).

state and international electricity trade. The failure to coordinate standards has been accompanied by a failure to integrate and coordinate renewable electricity certificate (REC) markets, which means that the full gains from trade of RECs are not realized. Most, but not all, states recognize "unbundled" RECs, credits whose trade is not attached to transmission of the underlying electricity. Recognition of unbundled RECs allows utilities to take credit for renewable electricity that is not actually transferred to the locality where the utility operates, widening the geographic area in which renewable energy can be generated to meet a state's standard. States that do not yet recognize unbundled RECs include Iowa, Arizona, and Hawaii.

Even within states that do recognize RECs from out of state, varying definitions of renewable energy limit the liquidity of REC markets, as a REC certified in one state might not be saleable to another state because it does not comply with the second state's standard. A standard North American definition of renewable energy would increase REC fungibility, ensuring that a credit created in one state or province could be used toward compliance with renewable standards in another part of the continent. In addition, the markets themselves should be coordinated; many state laws do not clarify which attributes RECs require in order to count toward compliance with renewable portfolio standards (Holt and Wiser 2007).

Another issue that could arise within the North American Free Trade Agreement (NAFTA) relates to the preferences that some state standards give to important state industries or conditions peculiar to the state. One of the more egregious examples of this trend is North Carolina's renewable portfolio standard, which requires providers to supply 0.2 percent of their portfolios from swine waste and 900,000 megawatt hours of electricity from poultry waste in 2018 (Horlick, Schuchhardt, and Mann 2002). This requirement indirectly subsidizes North Carolina's livestock industry and provides an advantage to electricity producers within the state with access to North Carolina's waste lagoons (Fickling 2010).

Many states exclude large hydropower altogether from qualifying as renewable electricity, a point that is highly contentious among states and provinces on the US-Canada border. Canada's electricity exports are significant—about 10 percent of Canadian generation—and most of these exports derive from large hydropower. Hydro-Québec has been a vocal advocate for including large-scale hydropower in state standards, arguing the case in New York state discussions and preparing a submission to the NAFTA Commission for Environmental Cooperation. Manitoba Hydro and the state of Minnesota have also clashed over the definition of hydropower in state standards (Rowlands 2009).

NAFTA Legality

Trade in electricity is subject to national treatment clauses under NAFTA Articles 301 and 606(1). By definition, renewable portfolio standards make distinctions between electricity produced from fossil fuel–based resources and electricity produced from renewable resources. This distinction potentially raises issues of discrimination among like products, as electricity has the same qualities regardless of the source. Under a renewable portfolio standard, electricity is regulated according to processes and production methods (PPMs), i.e., the manner in which the product is created and the resources used to create it. The issue at hand is whether PPMs may be considered in determining likeness under NAFTA. While PPM-based measures are not necessarily prohibited by international trade disciplines per se,[24] there is considerable uncertainty regarding the extent to which such measures are valid under NAFTA and General Agreement on Tariffs and Trade (GATT)/WTO disciplines.[25]

Other case law decided under GATT Article 3, however, seems to suggest that renewable electricity would not be treated as a like product under NAFTA dispute settlement. The WTO Appellate Body stated in *Japan–Taxes on Alcoholic Beverages* that "likeness" should be "construed narrowly"; the product's end use in a given market, nature and quality, and tariff classification, as well as evidence of consumer preferences and habits, may all be addressed in determining product likeness.[26] Public demand for renewable electricity could provide such evidence of differing consumer preferences; many utilities charge a premium for electricity produced from renewable sources (Howse and Van Bork 2005).

Even if renewable and nonrenewable electricity are considered to be like products, they would almost certainly be exempted from NAFTA national treatment provisions under GATT Article 20, which is incorporated into Article 2101 of NAFTA (Horlick, Schuchhardt, and Mann 2002). The renewable standard is clearly intended to "conserve . . . [a] natural resource," as clean air has been interpreted as such in *United States–Standards for Reformulated and Conventional Gasoline*. It also may fall under the exceptions of GATT Article XX(b) for measures "necessary to protect human, animal, or plant life or health."

Some state standards that favor certain kinds of renewable energy, however, might violate the chapeau of Article XX. Standards that favor solar generation, for example, could be viewed as "arbitrary," as solar power does not obviously confer greater environmental benefits than other renewable sources such as wind. On the other hand, the cost of solar could drop dramatically if the technology were scaled, and the fall in price could serve an environmental purpose by making solar power more attractive. Also potentially arbitrary are standards that create separate classes of renewable energy without adequate environmental justification for the creation of those classes. Standards that

---

24. See *United States—Import Prohibition of Certain Shrimp and Shrimp Products*, WT/DS58/AB/R, paragraph 121.

25. Dispute settlement could occur through a number of venues, including Chapter 20 panel consultations and possibly Chapter 11 dispute settlement (Horlick, Schuchhardt, and Mann 2002). See also Hufbauer and Schott (2005).

26. Appellate Body Report, *Japan–Taxes on Alcoholic Beverages*, WT/DS8,10,11/AB/R, adopted on November 1, 1996, 20-21.

discriminate against hydropower based on the size of the installation could face the same problem.

The counterargument would be that hydropower is a fixed resource that has already been commercially proven, and thus there is little environmental benefit to promoting additional investment. There is also a strong argument that large hydropower poses environmental difficulties unrelated to climate change and that exclusion of large hydropower would thus fall under Article XX(b) or XX(g). However, states might have to provide convincing evidence that such environmental difficulties impact the United States, as it is unclear whether Article XX applies to environmental effects confined to another jurisdiction.[27] If a NAFTA panel concludes that effects must be felt in the regulating jurisdiction, states may have to show that Canadian hydropower has a detrimental effect on their environment in order to justify the exclusion of imported hydropower (Horlick, Schuchhardt, and Mann 2002).

States that exclude out-of-state producers altogether from contributing toward compliance with renewable portfolio standards will face a much tougher case under a NAFTA panel. These states often justify excluding out-of-state providers by citing the need to develop renewable energy in state. While there is no reasonable environmental justification for restricting renewable development to in-state production on climate change grounds, as greenhouse gases spread easily across borders, there is perhaps a justification on air pollution grounds, as air pollution tends to remain most severe in the locality in which it is emitted. This line of reasoning, however, might be construed to conflict with the argument above that clean air and water are shared North American resources. Whether a NAFTA panel would recognize a need to develop in-state renewable resources remains to be seen.

In a broader sense, state renewable standards have not yet fallen into compliance with Article 904(6) of NAFTA, which states that "the Parties shall, to the greatest extent practicable, make compatible their respective standards-related measures, so as to facilitate trade in a good or service between the Parties." This provision would seem to indicate that states and provinces have a responsibility to harmonize their definitions of renewable energy in order to remove obstacles to renewable electricity trade. To be sure, it is not clear whether state renewable standards fall under the purview of NAFTA Chapter 9. Gary Horlick, Christiane Schuchhardt, and Howard Mann (2002) argue that technical regulations as defined under Article 915 might be limited to PPMs that relate to the products' physical characteristics. Such a definition would exclude regulations regarding renewable energy, which does not take on special physical characteristics regardless of the PPMs that are used.

___

27. This would seem to be a narrow interpretation, and the panel and Appellate Body in the WTO case *United States—Import Prohibition of Certain Shrimp and Shrimp Products* specifically avoided answering the question of whether there is an implied jurisdictional limitation in Article XX. By making the point that the endangered turtles in question swim through US waters, however, the Appellate Body acknowledged the possibility of such a limitation.

Low-Carbon Fuel Standards and Oil Sands Production

Approximately 30 percent of North American GHG emissions come from transportation. Efforts to reduce transportation's contribution to climate change have largely focused on the fuel efficiency of vehicles, but recent initiatives have also aimed to spur investment in renewable and alternate fuels. Among these efforts, the low-carbon fuel standard is the first to take a comprehensive, market-based approach. Unlike previous initiatives such as ethanol mandates and incentives to produce electric cars, the LCFS does not pick winners among technologies. Rather, it requires fuel distributors only to achieve a certain amount of carbon reduction per unit of fuel sold; distributors are free to accomplish this task in whichever manner is most effective.

In maintaining this focus on emissions reductions, the LCFS is a vast improvement on ethanol standards previously implemented at the federal level and in several US states. For example, the federal Energy Independence and Security Act requires a certain portion of the ethanol blended toward compliance with the law to achieve 20 percent GHG emissions reductions relative to conventional fuels, but a large loophole exempts 15 billion gallons of corn-based ethanol from this requirement (EIA 2008). Recent studies suggest that corn-based ethanol produced in the United States could be even more carbon intensive than gasoline itself (Crutzen et al. 2008, Searchinger 2008). By contrast, California's LCFS does not exempt corn ethanol from a requirement to reduce emissions, and California's regulations use a stricter analysis of land-use change from the growing of corn and other crops for fuel.

California and British Columbia are the only jurisdictions currently implementing an LCFS. However, Oregon is developing an LCFS, and Ontario and the RGGI region have committed to adopting the standard. WCI members, including Washington, are also considering adopting an LCFS, and the Midwest Greenhouse Gas Accord steering committee has discussed incorporating one into its program. President Obama has called for a national LCFS, but the provision was dropped from the American Clean Energy and Security Act.[28]

California Low-Carbon Fuel Standard

Executive Order S-01-07 instructs the CARB to develop and implement an LCFS that reduces the average carbon intensity of passenger vehicle fuels by 10 percent between 2010 and 2020. In order to comply with the LCFS, firms may blend or sell an increasing amount of low-carbon fuel or purchase credits from fuel providers that have exceeded the standard. Firms may also bank credits for use at a later date. A set of draft regulations requiring well-to-wheel life-cycle analysis to determine GHG content was released in October 2008,

---

28. If widely adopted, the LCFS probably would constrain imports from Canadian oil sands and encourage greater production of sugarcane, soy, and cellulosic ethanol and biodiesel.

and revisions were released in January 2009. Because the regulations ratchet down allowable average GHG content starting in 2011, new technologies must be implemented immediately in order to meet the standard.

A pitfall or a benefit of California's LCFS—depending on one's point of view—is that it will constrain oil sands imports into jurisdictions that adopt it. Depending on the benchmarks and assumptions used, oil sands production generates 13 to 26 percent more GHG emissions on a well-to-wheel basis than light crude, and 5 to 15 percent more than the average basket of fuels consumed in the United States (Toman et al. 2008, IHS CERA 2010).[29] This puts it at a disadvantage to conventional oil and other fuels under the standard, particularly as the cost of producing from the oil sands is already relatively expensive compared to conventional crudes. Oil sands operations could lower their carbon footprint to that of conventional fuels by using carbon capture and storage technology, but the technology has not yet been developed at commercial scale and will likely prove to be an expensive option, especially in the short run.

Treatment of the oil sands under climate legislation is possibly the single biggest—or at least the single most publicized—source of tension between the United States and Canada on climate change issues. Production and trade of oil sands fuel is important for both Canada and the United States, but the fuel also accounts for a large share of Canadian GHG growth over the past decade. Canada cannot meet its global GHG reduction commitments without slowing growth of GHG emissions from this sector. Because of the economic impact of reducing oil sands production, however, the Canadian government has been very skeptical of US efforts to target unconventional fuels in the design of fuel and emissions standards (see chapter 3).

However, some perspective is required. California consumes a very small portion of the oil sands products sold to the United States, and LCFS limited to California are likely simply to divert oil sands consumption to areas not covered by the standard (CARB 2009). Currently, the midwestern region of the United States purchases 70 percent of the oil exported from the Canadian oil sands; by contrast, the entire west coast region purchases only 4.5 percent.[30] As such, an LCFS limited to California is unlikely to have a significant deterrent effect on oil sands production.

An oil sands pipeline project to Wisconsin has been approved by the

---

29. The additional GHG emissions arise due to the carbon intensity of extraction and the process of upgrading bitumen. The GHG intensity of oil sands extraction varies between mining and in situ extraction. Oil sands production with mining is 13 to 22 percent more GHG intensive than light crude on a well-to-wheel basis, whereas production with in situ extraction is 19 to 26 percent more GHG intensive. Moreover, these emissions estimates depend on whether they are compared with light crude only or with the blend of light and heavy crudes consumed in the United States today. Heavy crudes produce more GHGs when upgraded; thus, oil sands appear less emissions intensive when compared with these fuels (Toman et al. 2008, IHS CERA 2010).

30. National Energy Board, Total Crude Oil Exports by Destination—Annual, www.neb-one.gc.ca (accessed on June 7, 2011).

US State Department, and others have been proposed in the Gulf Coast and Rocky Mountain regions. Such pipelines would potentially allow the oil sands to achieve even broader US market penetration.[31] In addition, the Canadian National Energy Board approved the Keystone XL pipeline project to the Gulf Coast in March 2009 but it has not yet cleared all US regulatory hurdles.[32] The pipeline appears to be supported by federal authorities in the State Department, which is responsible for approving it (US Department of State 2011). However, the EPA has repeatedly asked the State Department to examine the extra GHGs emitted in transporting and refining the oil.[33] In addition, a number of politicians have opposed the project on environmental grounds. Particular attention has also been given to the susceptibility of the proposed pipelines to spills,[34] and to the proposed routing of the pipeline over the Ogallala Aquifer, which supplies 80 percent of Nebraska's drinking water.[35] Due to the controversy, the State Department announced in March 2011 that it would open an additional public comment period and would reach a decision by the end of the year.[36]

If approved, the pipeline to the Gulf Coast could exacerbate the problem of carbon leakage created by a low-carbon fuel standard. The Gulf Coast is the largest refining market in North America and has ready capacity to process heavy crude. If the region's sparse record of climate change legislation is any indication, the Gulf Coast area will likely be one of the last regions to adopt an LCFS, providing a prime new market for Alberta's oil sands products should additional states follow California's lead.

Leakage might not be the only problem inherent in an LCFS. Canada has also raised questions about the compatibility of the LCFS with NAFTA obligations. The LCFS raises issues relating to discrimination among various fuel products on the basis of their carbon intensity and thus could possibly contravene national treatment obligations. Like the renewable electricity standard, the LCFS regulates based on PPMs, and it is not clear whether PPMs can be taken into account when determining "like" products. If PPMs are not a valid method of distinguishing between different products, then the conformity of

31. Steve Mufson, "State Department Gives Green Light to Canada-US Oil Pipeline," *Washington Post*, August 21, 2009.

32. Gordon Nettleton, Matthew Keen, and Ryan Rodier, "Canada: NEB Approves Keystone XL Pipeline Project: Market Forces Prevail as Key Public Interest Considerations," Osler, Hoskin, and Harcourt, LLP, March 28, 2010, www.mondaq.com (accessed on May 21, 2011).

33. Elana Schor, "EPA Seeks Expanded Review of Proposed Oil Sands Pipeline," *Greenwire*, June 7, 2011.

34. Kim Murphy, "One Oil Pipeline Too Many for Texas?" *Los Angeles Times*, January 24, 2011.

35. Lee-Anne Goodman, "US Set to Approve Keystone XL Pipeline," *Globe and Mail*, October 20, 2010.

36. Shaun Polczer, "U.S. Puts New Conditions on Keystone Review," *Calgary Herald*, March 16, 2011.

the LCFS with NAFTA obligations might turn on the applicability of exceptions in NAFTA Article 2101 and GATT Article XX.

Like the renewable portfolio standard and climate legislation more generally, the LCFS is intended to conserve natural resources and thus likely falls under Article XX(g). Depending on a NAFTA panel's interpretation, however, the LCFS may violate the GATT Article XX chapeau (which is incorporated into NAFTA) against "arbitrary or unjustifiable discrimination." At issue is the method used by CARB to calculate carbon intensity. The LCFS regulation creates two categories, alternative fuels and conventional gasoline; the latter consists of a basket of fuels that comprise 2 percent or more of California's crude mix. Conventional fuels are all assigned the same carbon intensity value, which is equal to the average carbon intensity of the conventional gasoline basket. By contrast, alternative fuels receive a separate carbon footprint analysis.

Whether this is a fair means of distinguishing "dirty" fuels from "cleaner" fuels is an open question, given that individual fuels in the conventional gasoline basket might approach the carbon intensity of oil sands crude but are assigned the same default carbon intensity as other conventional fuels.[37] The natural resources minister of Canada claimed in an April 2009 letter to California's governor, Arnold Schwarzenegger, that the recovery emissions of Californian heavy crude were "similar to or higher than the range of emissions associated with extracting oil sands crude" and suggested that California's treatment of heavy crude as a lower-carbon "conventional fuel" was discriminatory.[38] If a NAFTA case is brought and the dispute panel concurs that CARB's methodology disproportionately disadvantages the oil sands relative to other high-carbon fuels, the LCFS would be found in violation of NAFTA rules.

The fix for this would be one of two approaches: to apply a separate life-cycle value to every crude consumed in California, or to include oil sands in the basket of conventional gasoline, as Oregon has done (see below). Applying a separate life-cycle value would be administratively more difficult. By allowing producers to reduce their carbon intensity simply by substituting a marginally lighter crude for a heavier one, this approach would also encourage fuel swapping; that is, distributors selling across jurisdictions would have an incentive simply to sell their lighter crudes in California and their heavier crudes elsewhere.

This incentive could be avoided by including oil sands in the basket of conventional crude; this second approach would instead encourage producers to reduce carbon intensity by developing and disseminating new biofuels tech-

---

37. The Appellate Body ruled that different baselines for domestic and foreign gasoline violated national treatment in a separate case, *United States–Gasoline*. At issue in this case is whether a separate treatment for oil sands crude constitutes discrimination based on nationality or legitimate differentiation between the environmental characteristics of different products.

38. Government of Canada, Lisa Raitt letter to CARB, April 21, 2009, www.canadainternational. gc.ca (accessed on May 21, 2011).

nologies. A drawback to this approach, in climate terms, is that there would be little incentive for producers to avoid the use of higher-carbon synthetic fuels. However, by adjusting the carbon intensity of the conventional gasoline basket every couple of years, as Oregon has proposed, California's policymakers could ensure that higher emissions from an increased use of synthetic crudes would not swamp carbon reductions derived from an increased use of biofuels.

Proposed Oregon Low-Carbon Fuel Standard

Largely for administrative reasons, Oregon's proposed LCFS takes a different tack toward the oil sands than California's LCFS. Oregon's standard will not face the same legal challenges as California's as it treats all crudes equally. Under this proposal, Oregon will set one average carbon intensity for a basket of crude oils; the basket will include lower-carbon crudes as well as high-carbon crudes such as the oil sands. In order to account for likely oil sands growth and discourage the use of high-carbon crudes, Oregon will update the life-cycle value of the basket every three years. Thus, if distributors buy a higher share of oil from the oil sands, the recorded carbon intensity of the gasoline that they sell will increase after three years.

This approach goes only so far to discourage oil sands consumption, however. Because the average carbon intensity of gasoline will be calculated as a state-wide average, the incentive for each individual distributor to buy less fuel from the oil sands will be diminished. As a result, Oregon's standard has less severe implications for oil sands than California's standard.

State Initiatives Summary

In sum, states are pursuing various economy-wide and sectoral climate initiatives. All of these initiatives are patchwork in nature. Participation is largely limited to the coastal regions of the United States; even the most frequently adopted performance standard, the renewable portfolio standard, is mostly absent from the Southeast and Plains regions. State initiatives also show varying levels of coordination when it comes to their design. On one hand, states implementing cap-and-trade have formed multistate systems with broadly similar design features in each state. Renewable portfolio standards, on the other hand, are extremely diverse in their design, and there has been little effort to integrate these policies.

Carbon leakage is a concern with some state policies, such as the low-carbon fuel standard; it is less of a concern with regard to other policies, such as the renewable portfolio standard. Some state policies, such as California's cap-and-trade system, have been designed specifically with carbon leakage in mind; California will allocate allowances to carbon-intensive manufacturing industries in order to keep them from fleeing regulation by moving across the border. However, this is a short-term strategy. The optimal way to prevent leakage is to bring additional states into the fold, and coordination of state standards will therefore be crucial going forward. States implementing cap-and-trade thus face a major challenge: they must discourage additional states from exiting cap-and-trade pacts and bring in new partners. State cap-and-trade compacts already contain mechanisms for encouraging additional participation—but persuading reluctant states and provinces to join will not be easy given current political resistance to new environmental regulations.

In addition, performance standards, particularly renewable standards, could be helped along with coordination of infrastructure and policies. Because solar energy and wind energy are susceptible to intermittency—the amount of electricity generated depends on how much wind is blowing or how much sun is shining at the time—they need to be moved efficiently from areas where they are currently available to areas where they are needed. Thus, renewable installations spread over a large geographic area, with adequate transmission, enjoy economies of scale compared with renewable installations limited to a certain area, with poor transmission. Current transmission capacity for renewables is inadequate for the task. A Department of Energy study finds that wind power could constitute 20 percent of national electricity generation if, among other things, transmission capacity were significantly expanded (DOE 2008). Meanwhile, differing definitions of renewable electricity make it difficult to trade credits across regions, even though energy from a different region might achieve the common goal of reducing emissions. It is unrealistic to expect perfect agreement on definitions and targets for renewable energy, but more closely coordinated policies can help spur renewable development.

Finally, state standards face challenges when it comes to frictions with Canadian energy goals. Both the low-carbon fuel standard and certain renewable portfolio standards have been challenged by Canada for discriminating against Canadian energy. We discuss this issue further in the chapters to come.

Federal Climate Change Action

For the past two decades, federal climate policy has progressed in fits and starts. Support in Congress has been tepid at best; international climate initiatives often receive cautious if not skeptical comment. Although the United States signed the Kyoto Protocol, Congress never liked it, as indicated in the unanimous 1997 Senate vote on the Byrd-Hagel Resolution. After the terrorist attacks of September 11, 2001, and the war in Iraq, climate policy was subordinated to concerns about energy security and development of national fossil fuel resources. President Bush's 2001 Energy Task Force, which determined subsequent policy, focused much more on development than on conservation. Not surprisingly, US greenhouse gas emissions rose by 17 percent between 1990 and 2005.

In 2009, the Obama administration revived efforts to craft an integrated US climate policy. In June, the House of Representatives passed a cap-and-trade bill. The American Clean Energy and Security Act, sponsored by Representatives Henry Waxman (D-CA) and Ed Markey (D-MA), included a number of provisions aimed at building broad-based political support for a new carbon regime, including free allowances to major emitters and emissions offset provisions that help mitigate compliance costs. The bill set the goal of reducing emissions 20 percent by 2020 and 83 percent by 2050; its cap-and-trade component required covered sources to reduce emissions 3 percent by 2012, 17 percent by 2020 and 83 percent by 2050. Legislation stalled in the Senate, however, which rejected a bill largely based on ACESA. Appendix 2A summarizes the proposed programs.

As a consequence, the likely approach at the federal level, at least for the next several years, will involve some form of regulation by the executive branch—though the scope of such regulation may be circumscribed by conditions and funding constraints set by Congress. Many of these regulations would be implemented through the Clean Air Act, although appliance and efficiency standards might be enacted through the authority of the Department of Energy under the Energy Policy and Conservation Act.

Congress might also consider relatively limited legislative approaches in the near term. A federal clean energy standard along the lines of that proposed by Senator Richard Lugar (R-IN) in 2010 continues to enjoy bipartisan interest in Congress. Building standards, low-carbon fuel standards, and a legislative tightening of CAFE standards might also be introduced.

EPA Approaches

The Supreme Court ruled in 2007 that the Clean Air Act requires the EPA to regulate GHGs if they are found to endanger human health and welfare; in 2009 the EPA reached such a finding. The EPA has taken its obligation to regulate GHG emissions seriously. A week after the Senate abandoned hope of passing climate change legislation in 2010, the EPA issued a report affirming its position, declaring in a press release that "climate science is credible, compelling and growing stronger."[39] Nonetheless, the EPA has had to traverse political mine fields in the climate area. To ensure full consideration of public comments, the EPA postponed releasing certain draft GHG regulations from June 2011 until September 2011.[40]

EPA regulation of greenhouse gases comes at a time when regulations are being developed and augmented for a variety of different pollutants, such as mercury, NO_x, and coal ash. Combined, these regulations will likely have significant implications for coal-fired power plants—particularly older plants, for which implementing additional pollution controls may be uneconomical. However, all of these regulations, except for those on coal ash, are court ordered and have been in the pipeline for several years. As such, we view them

39. Environmental Protection Agency, EPA Rejects Claims of Flawed Climate Science, press release, July 29, 2010, http://yosemite.epa.gov (accessed on June 7, 2011).

40. Tennille Tracy, "EPA Delays Greenhouse-Gas Rules for Power Plants," *Wall Street Journal*, June 13, 2011.

as part of the "business as usual" case and limit our discussion in this chapter to EPA measures focused specifically on GHGs.

The Clean Air Act provides a variety of mechanisms for regulation, including the National Ambient Air Quality Standards (NAAQS), New Source Performance Standards (NSPS), and New Source Review (NSR). The EPA could also potentially regulate under Section 115 of the act, which requires the EPA to regulate pollutants that endanger health or welfare abroad, although this provision has never been used. Below, we describe each mechanism.

National Ambient Air Quality Standards

NAAQS allow the EPA to set, for certain "criteria" pollutants, maximum ambient pollution levels that must not be exceeded by any jurisdiction. The six pollutants currently covered under NAAQS were chosen because they endanger public health and welfare and because their presence results from several mobile and stationary sources. NAAQS require states to develop State Implementation Plans to bring themselves into compliance with the standard. These plans must be approved by the EPA, which has the authority to develop its own federal implementation plan if a state is unable to develop an adequate plan. Regulation is not limited to certain sources, as it is under some other Clean Air Act programs, but rather applies to the whole economy.

It might be possible for the EPA to implement an emissions trading system under NAAQS. It did so for the NO_x group of acid rain–causing pollutants after several states continually failed to achieve compliance with the EPA's NAAQS standard. The EPA implemented this program by publishing a model rule that states could choose to include in their implementation plans; all of the states chose to do so (Richardson, Fraas, and Burtraw 2010).

The problem with using NAAQS as part of a climate change policy is that they measure compliance in terms of whether pollution concentrations in each state fall under certain limits. Because GHG emissions spread throughout the globe and individual state emissions represent only a small fraction of global emissions, a state program on its own cannot effect a meaningful change in that state's GHG concentrations. The way NAAQS measure state "compliance" and "noncompliance" is thus meaningless when it comes to GHGs. Either the standards for ambient pollution concentrations will be set so loosely that all 50 states are in compliance, or the standards will be set at such a level that all states remain out of compliance.

If standards are set such that states remain out of compliance, states will be required to formulate State Implementation Plans to address climate change. This could spur states to reduce their GHG emissions, a positive outcome. Because NAAQS require the results of the implementation plans to be measured in terms of ambient pollution levels, however, they do not provide a good framework for assessment of these state programs. As a result, NAAQS are generally not regarded as the best approach for regulating greenhouse gases under the Clean Air Act.

Clean Air Act Section 115

Section 115 of the Clean Air Act is a short, never-used section directed at reducing US emissions that cause harm to human health or welfare abroad. In order for the EPA to regulate under Section 115, the affected countries must afford reciprocal treatment. Nathan Richardson, Arthur Fraas, and Dallas Burtraw (2010) argue that Section 115 is so vague and so buried within the text of the Clean Air Act that it is likely to be challenged successfully in court if it is used to justify regulation of greenhouse gases.

New Source Performance Standards

Under NSPS, the EPA may set technology-based standards individually for each industrial category. While the EPA generally does not specify the technologies that must be used, it does set performance standards that could be achieved through the use of best available control technologies (BACTs). These standards are periodically refined to reflect technological progress. Standards for new and modified sources are set at the federal level, and additional standards for existing sources can be set at the state level. As with NAAQS, state standards must be approved by the EPA, and the EPA has the power to set federal standards if the states fail to regulate adequately.

Unlike NAAQS, NSPS regulate specific sources of pollutants, not the pollutants themselves (Monast, Profeta, and Cooley 2010). As a result, NSPS allow the EPA to negotiate with stakeholders and tailor its response to different sectors. Jonas Monast, Tim Profeta, and David Cooley (2010) suggest that this flexibility could enable the EPA to use the cap-and-trade bills recently debated in Congress as a model for its approach, allowing EPA regulation to dovetail with a future climate bill should one be passed.

Emissions trading under NSPS could be feasible, although it rests on uncertain legal grounds. In order to implement a cap-and-trade system under NSPS, the EPA would have to establish that emissions trading itself is a BACT. Given that NSPS are technology based, this argument might be perceived by the courts as a stretch. The only example of an emissions trading program implemented solely under NSPS authority, a mercury emissions trading program, was rejected by a DC circuit court ruling, although for a reason unrelated to the legality of emissions trading under NSPS (Monast, Profeta, and Cooley 2010; Richardson, Fraas, and Burtraw 2010).

Permitting: New Source Review and Prevention of Significant Deterioration

As soon as a pollutant is regulated under the Clean Air Act, sources that emit that pollutant are subject to New Source Review (NSR)—even if they are different from the sources regulated under other programs. NSR requires new emissions sources and major modifications to existing sources to obtain permits. Within areas where air quality standards have been met, the Prevention of Significant Deterioration (PSD) program requires sources to show that they will not increase emissions above a certain threshold and that they use a BACT. Within areas where air quality standards have not been met, sources must offset emissions increases and install lowest-achievable emissions rate technology. The requirement for the sources to do so often leads to more stringent standards than NSPS (Richardson 2010).

Possibilities for Regulation of Greenhouse Gases

The World Resources Institute analyzed three different potential EPA regulation scenarios, ranging from weak action to implementation of a cap-and-trade program under the Clean Air Act: "lackluster," "middle-of-the-road," and "go-getter" (Bianco and Litz 2010). Emissions are reduced in all scenarios, but the lackluster and even middle-of-the-road scenarios do not reduce nearly enough emissions to meet the United States' Copenhagen targets. To reduce additional damage, much less mitigate the total level of GHGs, would require new regulations, such as efficiency and emissions requirements for power plants. The report recommends tighter appliance efficiency standards as well as CAFE standards of 50 miles per gallon (mpg) by 2030 in the middle-of-the-road scenario and 63 mpg in the go-getter scenario.

As noted above, congressional politics will likely constrain the executive branch's ability to act. In June 2010, Congress rejected a resolution sponsored by Senator Lisa Murkowski (R-AK) that would have preempted the EPA from regulating greenhouse gases at all; a similar proposal by Senator Jay Rockefeller (D-WV) to delay EPA action for two years was blocked as well.[41]

With Republican Party gains in November 2010 in Congress, the go-getter scenario seems dead and gone. Nevertheless, it is not unreasonable to expect the lackluster scenario and some parts of the middle-of-the-road scenario to be implemented. Since vehicle fuel economy standards have historically fallen under the purview of the executive branch, it could be feasible for the EPA and Department of Transportation to adopt middle-of-the-road vehicle standards, and stronger appliance standards also might not be overly controversial. However, for power plants—the largest emissions source by far—the EPA has not indicated it will try to push the ambitious approach that the World Resources Institute report details. Instead it has directed the states to set relatively modest standards for energy efficiency.

Richardson, Fraas, and Burtraw (2010) estimate that a modest NSPS program to increase efficiency of coal plants could reduce national emissions by 3 percent. Efficiency could be increased either by introducing a uniform reduction in heat rates or by taking out of service the plants that do not meet a strict minimum efficiency standard. NSPS with trading could reduce national

---

41. Whereas the Murkowski amendment would prevent the EPA from regulating greenhouse gases, the Rockefeller amendment is limited to stationary sources.

emissions by 4.6 percent. Meanwhile, Burtraw, Fraas, and Richardson (2011) estimate that cost-effective performance standards for all new and existing sources identified by the EPA's tailoring rule could reduce national emissions by up to 6.2 percent. Nicholas Bianco and Franz Litz (2010) estimate that EPA action combined with action from other federal agencies and state governments could reduce national emissions 5 to 12 percent, although the upper range of this estimate involves robust state participation in carbon reduction initiatives and ambitious federal measures that are probably beyond the scope of the government's current plans.

Near-Term Prospects for Federal Regulation

The federal government has already begun to regulate GHGs under the Clean Air Act provisions described above. Shortly after President Barack Obama took office, the EPA issued a proposed regulation requiring large new emissions sources and capacity additions to existing sources to obtain permits under its New Source Review program.[42] PSD permitting requirements for GHGs have applied since January 2, 2011, to sources that are required to obtain PSD permits for other emissions and whose construction or modification would increase GHGs by more than 75,000 tons of CO_2e per year. The EPA is also expected to release draft NSPS regulations for power plants in September 2011 and draft NSPS regulations for petroleum refineries in December 2011.[43] In September 2009, the EPA also finalized a GHG reporting requirement for sources emitting over 25,000 tons per year of CO_2e.

In November 2010, the EPA released its proposed BACT guidance for PSD permitting. The guidance is necessarily vague, but it does shed some light on the EPA's plans. Energy efficiency improvements are on the table, but the guidance document discourages states from requiring coal-fired power plants to switch to natural gas or biomass or implement carbon capture and sequestration.

Implications for North America

Competitiveness Concerns

Given the current nebulous nature of pending EPA regulations, it is difficult to quantify their likely impact on trade in energy and energy-intensive goods. Credit Suisse (2010) estimates that proposed EPA regulation of non-GHG pollutants would temporarily raise electricity prices by 0.5 to 1 cent per kWh as utilities adjust—likely not a large enough increase to have significant competi-

---

42. Environmental Protection Agency, EPA Rejects Claims of Flawed Climate Science, press release, July 29, 2010, http://yosemite.epa.gov (accessed on June 7, 2011).

43. Tennille Tracy, "EPA Delays Greenhouse-Gas Rules for Power Plants," *Wall Street Journal*, June 13, 2011.

tiveness impacts for most energy-intensive manufacturing sectors, although the cost of producing primary aluminum could increase by up to 2.5 percent.[44] Burtraw, Fraas, and Richardson (2011) point out that measures likely to be required by the EPA—cost-effective energy efficiency improvements, and some biomass cofiring—would likely have been the first methods adopted by utilities under a cap-and-trade system. Thus, the marginal cost of implementing these improvements is unlikely to exceed the cost of the proposed Waxman-Markey bill. Appendix 2A contains an analysis of this legislation.

Lack of Policy Coordination

It is easy to say what EPA regulations will not do for Canada and Mexico. For one, they will not provide a basis for the kinds of competitiveness provisions that were central to the Waxman-Markey and Kerry-Lieberman bills. Importers of goods and services will not have to purchase international allowances at the border. Likewise, the special treatment for trade-intensive manufacturing industries that had been included in the cap-and-trade bills attempted by Congress is less likely to appear within command-and-control regulation.

The lifting of the threat of border measures may come as a relief to Canada and Mexico. However, regulation by the executive branch is unlikely to foster the trilateral carbon market that would have been created by a cap-and-trade bill. Richardson (2010) notes that whereas the NAAQS system does use domestic offsets, it provides no basis for international offsets. Offsets must be produced by firms in the same nonattainment area in which they are used. A foreign jurisdiction by definition could not meet this criterion because US law does not apply to foreign jurisdictions. NSR and PSD permitting schemes, meanwhile, are technology-based performance standards that have no history of using offsets as part of their implementation. NSPS do provide for emissions trading systems, which could theoretically use international offsets. Because the statutory language of NSPS does not mention international emissions sources, however, such international offsets might not stand up in court if challenged (Richardson 2010).[45]

If Canada chooses to fulfill its Copenhagen commitment, the task of reducing emissions will become much more expensive to carbon-intensive industries without the option of trading allowances with the United States. This is because it will likely cost more for Canada to reduce GHG emissions than the United States. The US Energy Information Administration projects that Canada's carbon dioxide emissions will grow at 0.8 percent per year

---

44. The increase is calculated by the authors using data from Ho, Morgenstern, and Shih (2008) and Energy Information Administration, Retail Sales of Electricity by State by Sector by Provider, www.eia.doe.gov (accessed on June 7, 2011).

45. Firms have challenged other aspects of Clean Air Act GHG regulations that reduce costs for industry—notably, the tailoring rule limiting regulation to large sources—in order to try to force the EPA to scrap GHG regulations altogether.

between 2006 and 2030, under business-as-usual conditions. In contrast, US emissions are projected to grow by only 0.3 percent per year. Canada is also projected to have the highest carbon dioxide intensity among Organization for Economic Cooperation and Development countries in 2030 under business-as-usual conditions: 359 metric tons (mt) per million dollars of GDP. US carbon dioxide intensity in 2030 is projected to be 282 mt per million dollars of GDP (EIA 2010). The difference in projected GHG emissions growth is largely due to the projected growth of emissions from Alberta's oil sands.

Consequently, Canada needs to make greater reductions in business-as-usual levels than the United States in order to achieve a given percentage change in greenhouse gas emissions—a requirement that entails higher prices if it goes it alone. Allowance trading with the United States could lower allowance prices substantially (Sawyer and Fischer 2010, NRTEE 2011).[46] See chapter 3 for a full discussion of the benefits and costs to Canada of trading emissions with the United States.

Regulatory Uncertainty

The uncertainty inherent in EPA regulations poses another problem for Canada and Mexico. The regulations take the EPA into somewhat uncharted legal territory, and several states, firms, and organizations have challenged them in court. Canada in particular has expressed interest in harmonizing its regulations with those of the United States, in order to mitigate competitiveness impacts (see chapter 3). However, it is difficult for Canada to create regulations that align with those of the United States when the United States' main climate regulations stand a high chance of being struck down.

Some interstate coordination issues exist with EPA regulation. WCI and RGGI states have argued that their cap-and-trade programs should be accepted as a substitute for the EPA's Clean Air Act regulations (Burtraw, Fraas, and Richardson 2011). Such a deal would reward early action, encouraging other states to join these cap-and-trade regimes. However, it could also produce accusations of favoritism, mobilizing additional opposition to EPA regulations from other states. Many of the interior states that have not embraced cap-and-trade also happen to have less efficient coal-fired power plants (Burtraw, Fraas, and Richardson 2011).

Clean Energy and Energy Efficiency

A federal clean energy standard may be introduced in coming legislative sessions. Endorsed by President Obama in his 2011 State of the Union address,

---

46. Dave Sawyer and Carolyn Fischer (2010) estimate that absent allowance trading, the cost of emissions allowances in Canada will be twice as much as in the United States to achieve the same quantity of carbon emissions reductions; NRTEE (2011) estimates that the cost will be about 50 percent greater.

such a standard would require utilities to generate a certain percentage of electricity from low-carbon sources such as renewables, nuclear, or coal-fired generation using carbon capture and storage. Natural gas might also be included in such a standard.

There has also been a renewed focus by the federal government on nuclear power loan guarantees. After decades of stalled growth in nuclear generation, the Department of Energy in 2010 announced $8.3 billion in loan guarantees afforded to two new nuclear reactors being constructed in Burke County, Georgia, which were authorized under the 2005 Energy Policy Act. The 2005 bill provided a total of $18.5 billion for nuclear power loan guarantees, but none of the money has been disbursed. A loan to a third nuclear plant was contemplated, but negotiations broke down in October 2010 over the terms of the loan. (The Energy Department sought $880 million for the $7.6 billion guarantee, in order to compensate taxpayers in the event of a default.[47])

As with state renewable portfolio standards, Canada and Mexico could provide some electricity toward meeting the proposed clean energy standard, particularly if transmission capacity is improved. Neither country provides a large fraction of the electricity consumed in the United States as a whole, but imports are significant for some border states. Notably, Vermont receives almost 40 percent of its electricity from Québec, and North Dakota and Minnesota receive 12 percent of the electricity they consume from Manitoba.[48] Almost all of these imports are from hydropower sources. Likewise, Mexico could be a significant source of solar and wind energy to the southern US border states, although the lack of transmission capacity currently represents a significant barrier (see chapter 4).

However, the clean energy standard's aim is to create *new* renewable generation. If imported Canadian and Mexican power is allowed to meet this standard, some measure will probably be required to prevent foreign utilities from swapping exported renewable electricity for fossil fuel–fired power imported from the United States. In order to prevent this type of reshuffling, the three countries should coordinate their approach to the renewable standard.

Summary and Conclusion

Due to years of stalling and uncertainty regarding climate change at the federal level, a number of state and regional initiatives have taken the place of coordinated national action. National legislation will be difficult to achieve, as disparities in regional production and consumption complicate congressional efforts to reach consensus on comprehensive GHG regulations.

Major state programs include cap-and-trade, renewable electricity standards, and measures to reduce the GHG content of transport fuels. These state

47. Matthew Wald, "Fee Dispute Hinders Plan for Reactor," *New York Times*, October 9, 2010.

48. National Energy Board, Electricity Exports and Imports 2007, www.neb-one.gc.ca (accessed on May 16, 2011).

measures will provide a template for future federal action. In addition, federal regulations enacted by the EPA through the Clean Air Act provide a stopgap measure that could allow the United States to accomplish at least a portion of its Copenhagen target for 2020.

This patchwork of regulations provides opportunities in allowing other jurisdictions to emulate or join regulatory regimes. However, it poses risks in the form of carbon leakage and inefficiencies due to scattered incentives. Some state regulations also include unnecessary barriers to energy trade.

US regulatory uncertainty also presents difficulties for Canada and Mexico. Because there is no comprehensive US federal policy, any policy adopted by Canada or Mexico could have adverse competitiveness impacts. Yet waiting poses risks of its own. If the United States does adopt cap-and-trade in the future, Canada and Mexico will likely need to follow suit with their own climate policies in order to avoid border trade measures—and this task will be more expensive if they take no action on climate change between now and then.

In the meantime, both countries will need to shift focus from the trade impacts of US federal legislation to the trade impacts of state legislation. California's low-carbon fuel standard and state renewable portfolio standards contain provisions that could affect trilateral energy trade. Depending on their design and implementation, these state performance standards could either boost energy exports, as in the case of the renewable portfolio standard, or threaten energy exports, as in the case of the fuel standard. In order to continue to take advantage of the US energy market, Canada and Mexico will need to adapt to shifting state regulation.

Although some initiatives are unlikely to pose serious carbon leakage or competitiveness problems, others will probably require greater coordination in order to minimize incentives for reshuffling carbon-intensive electricity, fuels, and production across state lines. Harmonization of state and federal standards through NAFTA and other trilateral channels could stave off legal disputes and increase the efficiency and effectiveness of climate measures. We provide our suggestions for how to achieve this harmonization in chapter 5.

Appendix 2A Cap-and-Trade

Congress has vetted about a dozen cap-and-trade proposals in the past few years. Though none has been successful to date, policies that set a price per ton of GHG emissions remain the preferred option for reducing greenhouse gases from the economist's point of view. Analysts broadly agree that carbon pricing offers the biggest "bang for the buck" of lost GDP.

Currently, carbon pricing approaches appear to be a political nonstarter. Politics is fickle, however, and eventual economic recovery could bring a new push for a comprehensive climate change bill. We therefore believe it is worth looking at recent proposals, as they could serve as models for future approaches. Certain aspects of climate legislation, particularly the international competitiveness portions, have been consistently applied in past legislation and are likely to remain the same in future bills. We believe our analysis of the regional and international issues inherent to passing legislation of this kind is thus likely to remain relevant.

Broadly, cap-and-trade bills set out three main objectives: to cut emissions, alter the mix and use of energy sources, and subsidize the economic transition to a low-carbon economy. In previous proposals, most actions necessary for compliance with the bill would be subsidized via free allowances and auction revenues over the first decade or so. A plethora of rebates, tax credits, handouts, and allowance allocations were included to reduce the cost of the bill. Allowance allocations and auctions also were used to mitigate adverse trade competitiveness impacts on domestic industries and to compensate low-income families for cost increases.[49] In the Waxman-Markey bill, about a third of allowances were allocated toward mitigating electricity price increases. Most of these allowances were given to local distribution companies, which were mandated to pass on the savings to consumers in a lump-sum fashion. Based on EPA allowance price estimates, these allowances to electricity would be valued at $23 billion to $31 billion in 2012, and $28 billion to $37 billion in 2020.

Cap-and-trade programs can also use emissions allowances for direct international aid. Both the Waxman-Markey and Kerry-Lieberman bills dedicated a certain portion of allowances to international mitigation and adaptation assistance. The portion set aside in the Kerry-Lieberman bill was very small, but the Waxman-Markey bill donated the value of 5 percent of total allowances for

---

49. A maximum of 2 billion tons per year of emissions could also be offset in any given year. A quarter to a half of these offsets could be international. In order to reduce leakage, both the Waxman-Markey and Kerry-Lieberman bills required international offsets from more-developed, higher-emitting countries to be counted on a sectoral basis; that is, country-wide emissions baselines had to be set for certain industrial sectors, and only reductions below those baselines in those sectors could be sold as offsets. We estimate that allowable offsets could have amounted to 27 to 32 percent of the total compliance obligation for firms between 2012 and 2025. In practice, however, there probably would not be that many certified offsets available, particularly internationally.

this purpose, which would have totaled between $2.5 billion and $3.5 billion according to EPA allowance price estimates. The program would have required countries receiving assistance to set a national baseline for deforestation that produces net zero deforestation in 20 years.

Competitiveness Measures in the House and Senate Bills

There are two main worries expressed by US legislators with regard to international trade and climate change policy: carbon leakage and competitiveness. Predicated on the pollution haven hypothesis, which posits that pollution-intensive industries tend to migrate to areas with less environmental regulation, carbon leakage refers to the possibility that national climate legislation will not abate carbon-intensive production but rather shift it to unregulated jurisdictions. Unlike ordinary air pollution, whose effects tend to remain fairly localized, GHG emissions spread evenly throughout the globe regardless of where they were initially emitted. Thus, carbon leakage, to the extent that it occurs, will frustrate countries' attempts to forestall further climate change within their own localities.

Although it is often conflated with the concept of leakage, competitiveness refers to the ability of domestic carbon-intensive firms in a regulated area to maintain production relative to international firms that do not face the same level of climate regulation. In a broad sense, cap-and-trade aims to provide incentives for a shift away from carbon-intensive production within the regulated jurisdiction. In the short term, however, maintenance of important carbon-intensive industries such as steel, chemicals, and cement is crucial to building political support for a cap-and-trade bill. In order to retain the support of key constituencies, a cap-and-trade program must avoid the appearance of losing market share in these industries to countries abroad that fail to adopt similar climate legislation.

Gary Hufbauer, Steve Charnovitz, and Jisun Kim (2009) catalogue the recent carbon tax and cap-and-trade proposals introduced in the US House and Senate, showing that all of the bills introduced after July 2007 contain some type of competitiveness provision. The two carbon tax bills, the Save Our Climate Act sponsored by Representative Fortney Pete Stark (D-CA), and the America's Energy Security Trust Fund Act sponsored by Representative John Larson (D-CT), impose equivalent taxes on imports. Meanwhile, all of the numerous cap-and-trade proposals include an international reserve allowance program, many beginning between 2019 and 2025, or a requirement that importers purchase allowances at the border for greenhouse gases emitted during the manufacture of the imported products. The international reserve allowance program is generally scheduled to be implemented after the start date of the cap-and-trade program, under certain conditions. Although some form of competitiveness provision is probably necessary to secure Congressional support, these trade-related measures carry some risks.

Details of the international reserve allowance program were spelled out in the Waxman-Markey and Kerry-Lieberman bills. In both pieces of legislation, the program would be implemented for a sector if less than 85 percent of imports in that sector come from countries that were deemed to have taken comparable action under the bill, unless the president and Congress agree that such a program would be detrimental for the economy. In order to meet the bills' criteria for comparable action in a certain sector, countries would need to

- be party to an international treaty to which the United States is a party that includes a nationally enforceable emissions reduction commitment at least as stringent as that of the United States; or
- be party to a sectoral emissions reduction agreement including the United States; or
- have a greenhouse gas intensity for the sector equal to or less than that of the United States.

Under both bills, the following imports would be exempt from border allowance purchase requirements:

- imports from least developed countries;
- imports from countries responsible for less than 0.5 percent of global emissions and less than 5.0 percent of US imports in the sector; and
- imports from countries that have taken comparable action.

ACESA and the American Power Act included allowance rebates allocated to specified industries to compensate for costs imposed by the bill; the objective was to keep US industries on an equal footing with industries in countries that do not adopt a cap-and-trade program. Under the allowance rebate program, trade-vulnerable industries could receive a maximum of 15 percent of the total number of allowances created by the bill in 2014 and 2015, and 13.4 percent in 2016 and thereafter. Trade-vulnerable industries were defined as having an energy or GHG intensity of at least 5 percent and a trade exposure of at least 15 percent. In addition, industries with very high energy or GHG intensities—defined as 20 percent or greater—were also eligible for rebates. Forty-two industries emitting a total of 665 million tons of GHGs—about 12 percent of the total carbon cap in 2014—would qualify.[50] By 2020, the allowances given to these industries could be worth $11 billion to $15 billion per year, based on EPA allowance price estimates (table 2A.1). Allowances would be distributed in proportion to a firm's output for the two preceding years, and 100 percent compensation would be provided for both direct and indirect compliance costs based on average carbon intensity for the sector. Rebates were slated to end in 2035.

In calculating how many allowances importers must buy at the border, the

50. Trevor Houser, testimony before the Committee on Energy and Commerce, US House of Representatives, April 23, 2009.

Table 2A.1 Allowance distribution under HR 2454: American Clean Energy and Security Act of 2009 (Waxman-Markey bill)

Distribution	2012	2013	2014	2015	2016	2017	2018	2019	2020
	Allowances allocated and auctioned under Waxman-Markey bill (percent)								
Allocations									
Electricity consumers	43.8	43.8	38.9	38.9	35	35	35	35	35
Local distribution companies (approximate)	38.8	38.8	33.9	33.9	30	30	30	30	30
Trade-vulnerable industries (maximum)[a]	2	2	15	15	13.4	13.4	13.4	13.4	13.4
Other	26.8	25.5	29.3	29.3	35.1	34.8	34.8	34.8	35.1
Auctions									
Low-income consumers	15	15	15	15	15	15	15	15	15
Other	12.4	13.8	1.8	1.8	1.4	1.7	1.7	1.7	1.5
Total allocated	72.6	71.2	83.2	83.2	83.6	83.3	83.3	83.3	83.5
Total auctioned	27.4	28.8	16.8	16.8	16.4	16.7	16.7	16.7	16.5
Total	100	100	100	100	100	100	100	100	100
	Millions of allowances allocated and auctioned under Waxman-Markey bill (1 allowance = 1 ton CO_2e)								
Allocations									
Electricity consumers	2,066	2,021	1,947	1,903	1,868	1,823	1,778	1,733	1,671
Local distribution companies (approximate)	1,830	1,790	1,697	1,658	1,601	1,563	1,524	1,486	1,433

Trade-vulnerable industries (maximum)[a]	94	92	751	734	717	700	683	665	642
Other	1,268	1,177	1,466	1,433	1,874	1,814	1,769	1,724	1,674
Auctions									
Low-income consumers	708	693	751	734	800	781	762	743	716
Other	586	636	91	89	77	90	89	87	72
Total number of allowances	4,770	4,666	5,058	4,942	5,391	5,261	5,132	5,002	4,873
Strategic reserve	48	47	51	49	54	53	51	50	97
Allowances available[b]	4,722	4,619	5,007	4,893	5,337	5,209	5,080	4,952	4,775
Number of allowances allocated	3,428	3,291	4,165	4,069	4,459	4,337	4,229	4,123	3,988
Number of allowances auctioned	1,294	1,328	842	823	878	871	851	829	788
Estimated allowance price (EPA, 2005 dollars per ton CO_2e)									
Minimum	11	11.55	12.13	13	13.65	14.33	15.05	15.8	17
Maximum	15	15.75	16.54	17	17.85	18.74	19.68	20.66	22

(continued on next page)

Table 2A.1   Allowance distribution under HR 2454: American Clean Energy and Security Act of 2009 (Waxman-Markey bill) (continued)

Distribution	2012	2013	2014	2015	2016	2017	2018	2019	2020	Total, 2010–19
	Value of earmarked allowances/allowance revenues (millions of 2005 dollars)c									
Allocations										
Electricity consumers	26,859	27,584	27,910	28,541	29,418	30,147	30,876	31,602	32,592	265,530
Local distribution companies (approximate)	23,789	24,432	24,322	24,871	25,216	25,841	26,465	27,088	27,936	229,959
Trade-vulnerable industries (maximum)[a]	1,228	1,261	10,765	11,008	11,294	11,574	11,854	12,132	12,512	83,628
Other	16,478	16,071	21,017	21,492	29,515	30,005	30,713	31,435	32,652	229,378
Auctions										
Low-income consumers	9,209	9,457	10,765	11,008	12,608	12,920	13,233	13,544	13,968	106,712
Other	7,619	8,676	1,310	1,339	1,217	1,489	1,542	1,579	1,395	26,166

EPA = Environmental Protection Agency

a. Trade-vulnerable industries are those with energy or greenhouse gas intensity of at least 5 percent and a trade intensity of at least 15 percent. The amount of compensation for these industries is determined by a statutory formula. The values listed here are the maximum amounts of allowances, in aggregate, that may be provided for trade-intensive industries; they do not necessarily represent the amount that will actually be disbursed.
b. Equal to total allowances created less the total allowances for strategic reserve.
c. Calculated using the average of EPA's minimum and maximum allowance price estimates.

Sources: HR 2454: American Clean Energy and Security Act of 2009, available at www.govtrack.us; EPA (2009).

international reserve allowance program in both bills factored in the allowance rebates received by covered firms and free allowances to electricity. The border allowance purchase requirement could actually be as low as zero if it were determined that the allowance rebates granted to firms fully compensate for the costs imposed by the Waxman-Markey bill.

International Harmonization: Implications of Federal Legislation for NAFTA

Numerous provisions of past US legislative proposals, if implemented, would have implications for Canada and Mexico that could either encourage or impede North American cooperation on climate change. Several key issues merit attention.

International Competitiveness Provisions

First, cooperation could be dampened by the legislation's controversial approach to industrial competitiveness: a rebate system with a de facto border carbon tariff to be imposed in the not-too-distant future. It is not clear whether these competitiveness provisions would comply with WTO or NAFTA obligations.[51] Because the international reserve allowance provision in the Waxman-Markey and Kerry-Lieberman bills does not confer national treatment on imports, it would likely need to be justified under GATT Article XX, which is incorporated into NAFTA. GATT Article XX allows for measures "necessary to protect human, animal, or plant life or health" or "relating to the conservation of exhaustible natural resources if such measures are made effective in conjunction with restrictions on domestic production or consumption." The border measures would definitely fall into the second category, and probably would fall into the first as well.

However, measures must not be "arbitrary and unjustifiable discrimination," and case law to date suggests that a dispute settlement panel would place in this category the border allowance measure as laid out in recent bills. The Appellate Body in the *Shrimp-Turtle* case suggested that in order to comply with Article XX, measures must provide administrative flexibility to take into account different conditions in different WTO countries and must provide due process protections so that foreign firms are given an opportunity to appeal decisions regarding their ability to export to the United States. Though small emitters and least developed countries were automatically exempted from the border allowance purchase requirement, recent bills provided minimal administrative flexibility to respond to different conditions and contain no due process provisions.

Although the international reserve allowance program was largely targeted

---

51. For a thorough discussion of WTO rules regarding border adjustments, see Hufbauer, Charnovitz, and Kim (2009) and Maruyama (2010).

Table 2A.2   US imports of energy-intensive goods

Good	US imports from Canada and Mexico	US imports from world	US imports from North America
	Millions of US dollars		Percent
Steel	4,980	18,235	27
Cement	310	511	61
Paper	8,275	14,463	57
Aluminum	4,907	8,709	56
Chemicals	470	2,505	19

Source: US International Trade Commission Dataweb, www.usitc.gov (accessed on September 15, 2010).

toward developing country competitors, it is actually Canada that supplies much of the United States' carbon-intensive imports. Of the five most carbon-intensive manufacturing supersectors—steel, cement, paper, aluminum, and chemicals—Canadian imports rank first in all but the chemicals sector, in which they rank second. Canada supplies a majority of imports in the paper and aluminum sectors.[52] Mexico is also a major exporter of cement to the United States; in total, North America supplies over 60 percent of US imports in the cement sector (table 2A.2). Given the high level of trade integration in carbon-intensive manufacturing, the inclusion of the border allowance provision in US legislation has caused much consternation for the United States' North American neighbors.

It is unlikely that an international reserve allowance provision would be applied against Canada, for several reasons detailed in chapter 3. If the Waxman-Markey or Kerry-Lieberman bills had been enacted, Mexico might have proved to be a different story. Mexico has participated actively and in good faith in international negotiations and has made significant GHG reduction commitments compared with other developing countries; but the language of recent US legislative proposals does not appear to take into account different levels of development in determining which countries are subject to border measures. Absent any further clarification of the definition of "stringency," the decision about whether to hold developing countries to the same standard as developed countries would be left up to future administrations, subject to pressures from domestic interest groups. With billions of dollars of Mexican exports at stake, the issue of border measures could produce frictions between the two countries.

Though the rebate system has received less attention, it could also have trade-distorting effects. Because rebates are given out on a product-output basis, a rebate system could create perverse incentives to produce more goods

---

52. See chapter 3 for more detailed information on Canadian trade of carbon-intensive goods with the United States.

from the carbon-intensive sectors receiving the rebates. In earlier drafts of the Waxman-Markey bill, only 85 percent of costs to trade-vulnerable industries were subsidized. The congressmen's reasoning was that there is on average a 30 percent spread of carbon intensities in affected industries. With an 85 percent subsidy, therefore, the least carbon-intensive firms would have 100 percent of their costs subsidized; firms with average carbon intensities would have 85 percent of their costs subsidized; and the most carbon-intensive firms would have 60 percent of their costs subsidized. This proposal would have avoided overrebating any firm. In the version of the bill that passed the House of Representatives, however, firms with average carbon intensities would have 100 percent of their costs subsidized, and firms that were less carbon-intensive than average—half the industry in any given sector—would have over 100 percent of their costs subsidized. Because these subsidies would be given on a product-output basis, they would have the potential to be trade distorting.[53]

Perverse incentives in the bill would be muted by the fact that a two-year average of firm output is used as the basis for distribution. Nevertheless, Michael Dworsky, Marc Hafstead, and Lawrence Goulder (2009) estimate that the Waxman-Markey bill gave trade-vulnerable industries three times as many allowances between 2012 and 2030 as needed to retain the same level of profits. If the excessive rebates turned out to be trade-distorting subsidies, they could be successfully challenged in WTO dispute settlement.

Other analyses produce less extreme results. A 2010 interagency report estimates that net iron and steel imports would decrease by 0.6 percent as a result of the Waxman-Markey bill—an increase in the share of domestic production, but a small one (EPA et al. 2009). Even this small increase might not occur in reality, as the European Union also provides free allocations to market entrants, and firms in the European Union have an incentive not to shut down in order to keep their fixed allocations under the system. Even without measurable adverse trade effects, however, it is not clear whether the rebates would comply with Article 3.1(a) of the Subsidies and Countervailing Measures Agreement, which prohibits subsidies contingent upon export performance.

International Allowance Trading

Both the Waxman-Markey and Kerry-Lieberman bills contained international allowance trading provisions whose use could help link climate policies in North America. According to these bills, in order for US firms to use allowances "imported" from a foreign country, the foreign country would need to have a national or international carbon-trading regime that imposed mandatory greenhouse gas emissions limits on one or more sectors. The foreign cap-and-trade program would need to be at least as stringent as that of the United

---

53. Rebates could be smaller if the 15 percent maximum allocation of allowances for this purpose were insufficient to compensate firms for 100 percent of increased costs. An interagency report concludes that this is unlikely, however. See EPA et al. (2009).

States. For Canada, which would likely meet this standard, allowance trading with the United States could be a boon, halving the price of allowances and greatly mitigating pressures on carbon-intensive industries (see chapter 3).

While it is likely that Canada would meet this standard, it would be difficult for Mexico to comply in the near term. Nevertheless, there are other provisions of the Waxman-Markey bill that could facilitate Mexican participation in a North American carbon-trading regime through the sale of offsets (see below).

International Funding Provisions

In Copenhagen in December 2009, developed countries (led by Secretary of State Hillary Clinton) pledged $30 billion per year in funding available immediately for developing country climate change mitigation and adaptation efforts, to be scaled up to $100 billion per year by 2020. The Waxman-Markey bill contained several provisions that could have mobilized funds to meet the United States' share of the bargain. Based on EPA price estimates, we calculate that in 2012, between $3.6 billion and $5.0 billion worth of allowances and allowance revenues would be allocated to REDD, international clean technology deployment, and international adaptation, and that in 2020, between $5.7 billion and $7.4 billion would be allocated (table 2A.1). This money would not be nearly sufficient to meet the entirety of US funding pledges, but it would provide a significant start.

The Kerry-Lieberman bill, by contrast, did not allocate money directly to developing countries. Instead, it created the Strategic Interagency Board on International Climate Investment to coordinate funding for international climate activities from different federal agencies. Also, as mentioned above, the bill required the EPA and the Department of Agriculture to establish a program to provide assistance to reduce deforestation in developing countries; the goal of this program was to reduce GHG emissions by 720 million tons CO_2e in 2020 and 6 billion cumulative tons CO_2e by 2025. However, no funds were explicitly dedicated to this endeavor.

The significant portion of international offsets allowed under ACESA and the Kerry-Lieberman bill could have provided a channel for US support for GHG mitigation in Mexico, if Mexican firms proved responsive to price incentives to reduce emissions significantly below business-as-usual levels. Used properly, offset markets could improve the environment, reduce deforestation, alleviate poverty, and lower the cost of abating climate change. However, offsets require rigorous monitoring, reporting, and verification (MRV) in order to ensure that they represent genuine emissions reductions. Institutional cooperation would be required if MRV, and by extension offsets, were to be successful.

Due to its relatively high GHG emissions level and relatively high GDP, Mexico would likely have been required to sell offset credits on a sectoral basis in sectors covered under Waxman-Markey's cap-and-trade program. This means that for sectors covered under cap-and-trade, only emissions reductions under a countrywide baseline could be sold. Both bills required baselines to be established below business-as-usual trajectories; the Kerry-Lieberman bill in the Senate required baselines to "produce significant deviations" from business-as-usual levels. REDD credits could also be issued to Mexico for emissions reductions only under a countrywide baseline; these baselines would be established according to nationally appropriate mitigation actions and would be required to achieve net zero deforestation in twenty years. Mexico would be able to participate in a North American offset trading regime only if it were willing to set such baselines, and if firms were able to take actions to reduce emissions below those levels.

Regional Distribution Issues under a Cap-and-Trade Scheme

As we discussed earlier in chapter 2, the regional impacts of cap-and-trade are also important. Here, much depends on the way the cap-and-trade program is designed. James Boyce and Matthew Riddle (2009) model a cap-and-dividend program and find that the gross absolute cost of higher fossil fuel prices per capita varies from $239 in Oregon to $349 in Indiana. Increased costs as a percentage of income vary from 1.4 percent in Connecticut to 2.4 percent in West Virginia. But this variation is dwarfed by the variation among income deciles, and is partly explained by differences in income. For example, West Virginia households would bear a slightly lower absolute price burden per capita than Connecticut households; however, their incomes are 25 percent below the national average, so their price burden would be felt more heavily. On the other hand, repayment to the consumers in terms of equal dividends would cancel out the regressivity of this tax, and would smooth out variation among states in price burden per unit of income. If 100 percent of revenues are returned to consumers, average household impact as a fraction of income would vary from a 0.2 percent benefit in Indiana to a 0.9 percent benefit in Oregon.

This analysis applies only to aggregate economy-wide emissions, however. A carbon price could have far more disparate effects on electricity prices among states if steps were not taken to compensate households in certain regions. Although variation of overall emissions is relatively small, emissions per capita from electricity vary widely. Using state emissions intensity estimates cited by Boyce and Riddle (2009), we calculated that emissions from residential electricity consumption per capita range from 0.2 tons CO_2 in Vermont to 7.6 tons CO_2 in North Dakota; the national average is 3.0 tons CO_2. The cost per person of a modest $20/ton CO_2 price, prior to any sort of rebating mechanism and absent any fuel switching or energy-efficiency measures, would thus range from $5 per year in Vermont to $152 per year in North Dakota (see table 2A.3).

To address this regional equity problem, cap-and-trade systems may allocate allowances to local electricity distribution companies in order to offset electricity price increases. In contrast to electricity generators, which would

Table 2A.3 Carbon content of electricity consumption by state

State	Carbon intensity of electricity consumption (kilograms of CO_2/megawatt hour)	2008 residential electricity consumption (gigawatt hours)	Residential emissions from electricity per capita (tons of CO_2)	Annual cost per capita at $20 per ton CO_2
Alabama	669	32,185	4.7	94
Alaska	546	2,129	1.7	33
Arizona	558	33,236	2.8	56
Arkansas	630	17,392	3.8	76
California	454	91,231	1.1	22
Colorado	913	17,720	3.3	67
Connecticut	412	12,730	1.5	29
Delaware	933	4,428	4.7	93
District of Columbia	734	1,897	2.6	53
Florida	672	113,937	4.0	80
Georgia	708	55,587	4.1	82
Hawaii	857	3,085	2.0	39
Idaho	459	8,540	2.6	52
Illinois	556	46,780	2.0	40
Indiana	1,041	33,980	5.5	111
Iowa	933	14,073	4.4	87
Kansas	918	13,392	4.4	88
Kentucky	1,002	27,562	6.5	130
Louisiana	745	28,846	4.7	93
Maine	455	4,351	1.5	29
Maryland	681	27,144	3.1	63
Massachusetts	648	19,638	1.9	38
Michigan	666	34,297	2.2	44
Minnesota	780	22,355	3.2	64
Mississippi	631	18,294	3.9	78
Missouri	899	35,390	5.4	107
Montana	765	4,669	3.7	74
Nebraska	780	9,749	4.3	86
Nevada	702	12,061	3.1	63
New Hampshire	387	4,394	1.2	25
New Jersey	474	29,111	1.5	31

(continued on next page)

Table 2A.3   Carbon content of electricity consumption by state
(continued)

State	Carbon intensity of electricity consumption (kilograms of CO_2/megawatt hour)	2008 residential electricity consumption (gigawatt hours)	Residential emissions from electricity per capita (tons of CO_2)	Annual cost per capita at $20 per ton CO_2
New Mexico	935	6,379	3.0	60
New York	442	49,034	1.1	22
North Carolina	618	55,740	3.7	74
North Dakota	1,134	4,259	7.6	152
Ohio	852	53,411	3.9	79
Oklahoma	790	21,861	4.8	96
Oregon	227	19,910	1.2	24
Pennsylvania	613	54,060	2.6	53
Rhode Island	550	3,043	1.5	30
South Carolina	442	29,727	3.0	59
South Dakota	631	4,406	3.5	71
Tennessee	645	41,947	4.3	87
Texas	729	127,712	3.8	76
Utah	1,028	8,786	3.5	70
Vermont	73	2,133	0.2	5
Virginia	645	44,597	3.6	72
Washington	160	36,336	0.9	18
West Virginia	948	11,763	6.1	122
Wisconsin	840	21,976	3.2	64
Wyoming	1,099	2,719	5.7	115
United States	667	1,379,981	3.0	60

Sources: Boyce and Riddle (2009); EIA (2010); EIA, US Electric Power Industry Estimated Emissions, http://eia. doe.gov (accessed on July 10, 2010); US Census Bureau, Population Estimates, www.census.gov (accessed on July 10, 2010).

likely use such allowances to generate windfall profits, local distribution companies are regulated and are required to pass on the value of allowances to consumers in the form of cost savings. Modeling a 20 percent reduction in emissions by 2020, Anthony Paul, Dallas Burtraw, and Karen Palmer (2008) show that the distributional effects of allocations to local distribution companies (LDCs) depend on whether the allowances are apportioned based on population, historical emissions, or historical sales.

An apportionment scheme based on population would benefit regions such as the Pacific Northwest and the Northeast, which would receive more allowances than necessary, rewarding them for prior policies to improve energy efficiency and develop renewable energy. Under such a scenario, prices in California would actually decrease by 0.9 cents per kWh; the price increase in the Midwest due to climate policy would be mitigated but would still amount to 0.4 cents per kWh (Paul, Burtraw, and Palmer 2008). By contrast, an apportionment scheme based on historical emissions would virtually eliminate cost increases for midwestern and southeastern consumers, producing large price declines in Kentucky, West Virginia, and Indiana, but would increase costs for California and the RGGI region. In northern New England, prices are modeled to increase by almost 1 cent per kWh under this approach—almost as much as the largest price increase experienced by any region under full auctioning. Apportionment based on historical sales provides a middle ground between the two approaches.

Both the Waxman-Markey and Kerry-Lieberman approaches allocated a portion of allowances to local distribution companies. In the Waxman-Markey bill, the proportion of total allowances set aside for this purpose was roughly equivalent to the proportion of US emissions from electricity; 50 percent of these allowances were apportioned based on historical emissions, and 50 percent were apportioned based on historical sales. The Kerry-Lieberman bill was more generous to the midwestern and southern states, allocating 75 percent of LDC allowances based on historical emissions and the rest based on historical sales. Because utilities would receive allowances partly in proportion to their historic emissions, this scheme would somewhat level the playing field among regions that have already adopted clean energy and energy-efficiency measures and regions that have not. According to the bill, the value of these allowances would be passed on to consumers in a lump-sum fashion. Based on EPA allowance price estimates, allowances to electricity in the Waxman-Markey bill would be valued at $27 billion in 2012 and $33 billion in 2020 (see table 2A.1).

These efforts could have helped states with more carbon-intensive electricity production adapt to a carbon-constrained economy. Depending on the extent to which they reduced the transparency of the price signal, however, they could also have reduced financial incentives for residential electricity consumers to make energy-efficient home improvements. Responsiveness of individual families would depend on the extent to which the average family considered total electricity costs as opposed to marginal electricity costs when making decisions regarding energy-efficiency improvements. Dallas Burtraw, Margaret Walls, and Joshua Blonz (2009) find that the free allocation of allowances to LDCs would lower household income by up to $157 per household per year, assuming that families did not factor the increased marginal cost of electricity into consumption decisions, and that it could place more of a burden on lower-income households. Paul, Burtraw, and Palmer (2008) also find that the price of emissions allowances would increase by up to 13 percent due to the failure of customers to respond to electricity price incentives. In order to correct for this problem, Burtraw, Walls, and Blonz (2009) suggest allocating 15 percent of allowances to residential consumers only and returning the rest as a per capita dividend, a solution that would alleviate distributional inequities among households while still preserving some of the efficiency of a cap-and-dividend approach.

3

Canada

Canadian policy on climate change faces a difficult balancing act as it negotiates between competing demands—to exploit the country's natural resources and to contribute to international efforts to reduce greenhouse gas (GHG) emissions. This internal debate cuts two ways: It divides the western provinces, with large energy and agricultural production, from the manufacturing and maritime eastern provinces; and—since the provinces have jurisdiction over resource policies—it complicates federal-provincial policy coordination. No wonder it took years for Canada to formulate a national climate change policy; and even when it did so in 2000, the Federal Action Plan only modestly aspired to meet one-third of Canada's Kyoto target (Government of Canada 2000).[1]

Like its North American Free Trade Agreement (NAFTA) partners, Canada has recorded a sharp increase in GHG emissions over 1990 levels, despite its commitment to achieve a 6 percent reduction from these levels during the commitment period specified under Kyoto, 2008–12. By 2005, Canada's emissions were 27 percent above 1990 levels.[2] Almost 25 percent of Canada's increase in greenhouse gas emissions between 1990 and 2008 came from fossil fuel mining and production, much of which resulted from the rapid development of Alberta's oil sands (Environment Canada 2010).

Canadian federal climate policy is currently in flux. The policy environment has changed significantly since 2007, when the government issued Turning the Corner, a detailed plan to enact an intensity-based cap-and-trade

---

1. The plan relied heavily on forest and agricultural carbon sequestration and international offsets and proved ineffective in the face of rapid exploitation of new territories and expansion of oil production.

2. World Resources Institute, Climate Analysis Indicators Tool, 2009, http://cait.wri.org.

system coupled with some additional measures. With the ebb and flow and ebb of US legislative efforts, however, the Harper government has adopted a wait-and-see approach, pledging to harmonize Canadian policies with those of the United States but deferring major initiatives until the United States has a program in place.

To a large extent, the Canadian government has established itself as a policy taker in relation to the United States, due to the United States' potential to be either a significant asset to Canada's policy or a significant hindrance to its growth in certain industries. Emissions trading with the United States could greatly lower the cost of compliance with climate policy for energy-intensive Canadian firms and could enable Canada to take on more stringent commitments than would otherwise be feasible. Conversely, Canadian politicians worry that, without US action on climate change, the competitiveness of Canadian firms will be significantly disadvantaged if Canada pursues a unilateral climate policy. The Harper government is also concerned that trade-related measures in future US legislation could adversely affect Canadian industries.

Many provinces, however, have taken a different approach to climate policy. Legally and politically, Canadian provinces have more power to chart their own course on the environment than do US states, and provinces have a long history of steering environmental policy. Several provinces have used this power to implement cap-and-trade programs, carbon taxes, and performance standards.

This chapter will first detail the federal and provincial policies in place and under development, with an eye toward potential frictions. It will then discuss some of the challenges of harmonizing federal and provincial climate legislation while accommodating regional interests.

Federal Policy

In 2007, after a decade of indecision on climate change, the Canadian government published a set of climate change rules as part of its *Turning the Corner: Regulatory Framework for Industrial Greenhouse Gas Emissions* (Turning the Corner plan). These rules would be applied pursuant to the 1999 Canadian Environmental Protection Act (CEPA). The proposal targeted major industrial sectors and upstream sources of energy such as oil, gas, and electricity, requiring these entities to reduce their emissions intensity—emissions per unit of output—18 percent from 2006 levels by 2010, and 2 percent per year thereafter. However, fixed process emissions from industry were not given a reduction target until sufficient technology was deemed to have been developed. The plan required new and existing facilities to meet specified targets for emissions intensity. Alternatively, firms could contribute to a technology fund to cover a share of their emissions obligations at the rate of C\$15 per ton from 2010 to 2012, escalating to C\$20 per ton in 2013 and indexed to inflation thereafter. Firms could meet 70 percent of their obligations through the technology fund in 2010, phasing out to 0 percent by 2018. This fund was intended to serve as a de facto price cap in the early years of the program.

Domestic offsets were expected to play a large role in Canadian legislation. Offsets were limited to projects that began to achieve their emission reductions or removals after January 1, 2000, and only those emission reductions or removals that take place after January 1, 2008, could generate credits. Canada's regulatory framework did not set a cap on use of offsets. International offsets in the form of certified emissions reductions from the Clean Development Mechanism of the Kyoto Protocol, however, were limited to 10 percent of a firm's compliance obligation.

The Canadian government has backed away from Turning the Corner since its release, however, promising to significantly alter its plan in order to keep in line with US targets and to protect the competitiveness of Canadian industries. In its January 2010 Copenhagen submission, Canada pledged to reduce emissions 17 percent below 2005 levels by 2020 (in contrast to Turning the Corner's target of 20 percent by 2020); this new target was in line with the United States' Copenhagen promise and US legislation then being vetted in Congress. Canada has explicitly indicated that its submission is "to be aligned with the final economy-wide emissions target of the United States in enacted legislation" (UNFCCC 2010b).

The Canadian government has held to its position of policy harmonization even as the US federal government has dramatically scaled back its proposals on climate change. In a January 2011 speech, Environment Minister Peter Kent reversed the Harper government's position on cap-and-trade, calling instead for sector-specific regulations on energy-intensive industries. Specific attention was given to proposed US Environmental Protection Agency (EPA) regulations of greenhouse gas. Kent indicated that Canada would align with the EPA "where appropriate."[3]

Canada has already harmonized its climate change policies with those of the United States in the area of vehicle GHG emissions. Its new automobile standards for years 2011–16 were developed with the Environmental Protection Agency to conform to the US standards enacted in 2009. As in the United States, the new regulations require new cars to achieve a 25 percent reduction in GHG emissions from 2008 levels by 2016.[4]

Provinces: Independent Actors

Canadian provinces generally act much more independently of the federal government than do US states, and they have historically exercised a great deal of autonomy in environmental affairs. The 1867 Constitution Act delegates jurisdiction over natural resources and commerce to the provinces, and the

---

3. Peter Kent, Climate Change Milestones, speech at Economic Club of Canada, Toronto, January 28, 2011.

4. Kyle Danish, Shelley Fidler, Kevin Gallagher, Megan Ceronsky, and Tomás Carbonell, "Weekly Climate Change Policy Update—October 11, 2010," Mondaq, www.mondaq.com (accessed on May 21, 2011).

large geographic areas covered by most provinces have historically limited cross-border conflicts, so the federal government has largely stayed out of environmental regulation. While the Canadian government has enacted national environmental legislation, provinces generally take control of standards, permitting, inspection, and enforcement (Rabe 1999).

Accordingly, CEPA allows for equivalency agreements with provincial plans. The Constitution Act grants provinces jurisdiction over natural resources and the exclusive authority to make laws regarding property and civil rights. Under CEPA, the provinces retain jurisdiction over enforcement of environmental legislation and are allowed to adopt more stringent measures, but the federal legislation provides a floor; provinces cannot adopt standards that are less stringent than federal measures. In order for a province to enact regulation independently of the federal government, an equivalency agreement must be signed certifying that the provincial regulation surpasses the policy floor provided by federal regulation. Alberta is currently the only province that has signed an equivalency agreement with the federal government; the agreement covers pulp and paper, secondary lead smelter releases, and vinyl chloride releases.[5]

Provinces' historical jurisdiction over environmental policy could complicate integration of climate policy under a federal cap-and-trade program, particularly given the diversity of provincial programs in place or under development. In particular, controversy could arise over the federal government's allocation of revenues. As discussed later in the chapter, if the government fails to allocate the revenues to provinces in proportion to the provinces' emissions intensities, then a carbon-pricing policy will likely cause the western Canadian provinces disproportionate economic harm. Provinces, particularly in the west, are likely to demand that the revenue be returned to them.

Most of the provincial programs, rules, and performance standards to reduce greenhouse gas emissions are currently uncoordinated, though this lack of coordination is beginning to change. Manitoba and Ontario have proposed an east-west power grid in order to transmit renewable electricity more efficiently. Several provinces have committed to harmonize vehicle fuel efficiency standards with California, and British Columbia and Ontario have signed memoranda of understanding committing to adopt California's low-carbon fuel standard (LCFS). Four provinces—British Columbia, Manitoba, Québec, and Ontario—are part of the multijurisdictional Western Climate Initiative (WCI). Still, roadblocks to coordinated climate action remain. In particular, provincial promises of cap-and-trade face an uncertain future, and provincial cap-and-trade pacts could end up being much smaller than originally planned.

Canada does not have a province that clearly sets the pace on climate change, unlike the United States, where California tends to be the first to implement programs that are then closely emulated by other states. While US state regulatory regimes tend to fall into a few established categories—cap-and-trade systems, vehicle standards, fuel standards, and renewable portfolio

---

5. The agreement covers air pollution and not greenhouse gases.

standards—Canadian programs tend to be more diverse. Canadian provincial economy-wide greenhouse gas reduction programs, for example, embrace a wider variety of mechanisms than the cap-and-trade systems used in the United States by the Regional Greenhouse Gas Initiative (RGGI), California, and the federal government. Moreover, electricity standards in Canada include a variety of different performance requirements that are not generally found in the United States. Below, we summarize the provincial legislation implemented in Canada to date.

Economy-Wide Carbon Reduction Programs

Two provinces currently have well-developed economy-wide greenhouse gas reduction programs in place: Alberta and British Columbia. British Columbia, Québec, Ontario, Saskatchewan, and Manitoba have passed legislation authorizing cap-and-trade programs. In addition, Ontario and British Columbia have issued proposals for a provincial cap-and-trade system. Some of these programs, such as Alberta's intensity targets and British Columbia's carbon tax, are already being implemented. Other programs face a considerable degree of uncertainty. The future of Ontario's cap-and-trade program depends heavily on the outcome of the October 2011 provincial elections, and the rapid development of natural gas in British Columbia casts doubt on its cap-and-trade program.

Below, we detail the economy-wide carbon reduction programs in place and under consideration.

Alberta. Of all the provincial systems, Alberta's most resembles the federal government's Turning the Corner proposal. Regulation is limited to large industrial facilities producing over 100,000 tons of CO_2 equivalent (CO_2e) per year. By the end of 2007, "established facilities" were required to have reduced emissions intensities by 12 percent relative to the average of 2003–05 levels. New facilities must reduce intensity by 2 percent per year, after a three-year grace period. Like the federal proposal, Alberta's cap-and-trade system does not regulate industrial process emissions, although these emissions are included in the calculation that determines whether a facility exceeds the 100,000 ton CO_2e threshold for regulation. The government of Alberta has also committed C\$2 billion to development of carbon capture and storage (CCS) technologies.

As in the federal program, emitters also have the option of contributing a compliance payment of C\$15 per ton into a technology fund in lieu of reducing emissions or buying emissions credits. Unlike the federal program, however, this payment does not increase or phase out, meaning that the technology fund provides a C\$15 per ton price cap on emissions allowances. In the plan's first year of operation, only half of the emissions reduction target was reached; the other half was met through payments into the fund.[6]

6. Pembina Institute, "Alberta Industry Fails to Reduce Greenhouse Gas Pollution," May 2, 2008, www.pembina.org (accessed on February 17, 2009).

Because Alberta's climate program is structurally similar to the federal proposal, the federal government could make a deal with the province stipulating the emissions reduction targets at the federal level but allowing Alberta jurisdiction over the revenues collected. The price of payments into Alberta's technology fund could be adjusted to meet the price of payments into the federal fund. The feasibility of this equivalency agreement depends upon the extent to which the federal climate change regulation eventually implemented deviates from Turning the Corner.

British Columbia. British Columbia is the first and only jurisdiction in North America to have instituted a comprehensive carbon tax.[7] The tax started at C$10 per ton on July 1, 2008, and is scheduled to rise by C$5 per ton per year to C$30 per ton in 2012. All fossil fuels sold in the province are taxed at the wholesale level, except for marketable natural gas and propane, which are taxed at the retail level. Independent consulting company M. K. Jaccard and Associates projects that the tax will reduce greenhouse gas emissions by 3 million metric tons of CO_2e annually by 2020.[8] All of the revenue from the carbon tax will be refunded via tax cuts, two-thirds of which will go to individuals and one-third of which will go to businesses. In order to assist consumers with rising costs, a one-time C$100 climate action dividend will also be paid to every British Columbia citizen, and low-income people will receive a specifically designed tax credit.

British Columbia's Bill 18 provides the framework for a cap-and-trade system, including government-approved offsets and allowance trading with other jurisdictions (Ezekiel and Wilson 2008). A consultation paper released in October 2010 proposes three-year compliance periods, harmonization of allowance allocations with other WCI members, early reduction allowances for sources that reduce emissions prior to the 2012 start date, allocation of allowances to support research on renewables and CCS, and the use of offsets in accordance with WCI guidelines (BCMOE 2010).

Some firms have voiced concern over the competitiveness impacts of the proposed cap-and-trade system; in particular, they are concerned that the carbon tax and cap-and-trade program will not be sufficiently coordinated to avoid double taxation.[9] The government of British Columbia has indicated that measures will be taken to prevent this outcome, but it is not yet clear how the two regulations will be integrated.[10] In addition, a recent change of

---

7. Québec has also introduced a nominal carbon tax, but its sole purpose is to raise revenue; the tax is too small to change behavior.

8. British Columbia Ministry of Finance, "How the Carbon Tax Works," www.fin.gov.bc.ca (accessed on May 21, 2011).

9. Scott Simpson, "Business Council Urges 'Pause and Re-set' on British Columbia Cap and Trade Regs," *Vancouver Sun*, December 14, 2010, www.vancouversun.com (accessed on May 6, 2011).

10. Selina Lee-Andersen, "Towards an Emissions Trading System: B.C. Releases Consultation Papers for Cap and Trade Regulations," Blakes LLP, *Blakes Bulletin*, October 27, 2010.

leadership combined with rapid development of natural gas in the province led the government to revisit the previous government's cap-and-trade proposal in light of its economic impacts.[11] As of the writing of this chapter, it is not clear whether the proposal will go forward or whether substantial changes will be made to its scope.

Québec. Bill 42 authorizes Québec to create a cap-and-trade system. The legislation calls for interprovincial and interregional harmonization and allows reduction targets and emission caps to vary by sector. The bill also provides for wide coverage, encompassing any person or entity that operates a business, facility, or establishment that emits GHGs; distributes a product, the production or use of which involves emitting GHGs; or is specifically covered by future regulations. The first stage of Québec's cap-and-trade program, beginning in 2012, will cover GHG emissions from electric companies and heavy industry; the second stage, beginning in 2015, will target other industry sectors, including transportation and heating companies.

Saskatchewan. Saskatchewan's Bill 126, which also authorizes cap-and-trade, likewise fails to specify emissions reductions targets. However, draft implementing regulations envision an absolute economy-wide reduction target of 20 percent by 2020.[12] The bill creates four special nonprofit corporations: the Saskatchewan Technology Fund Corporation, the Saskatchewan Climate Research and Development Corporation, the Saskatchewan Climate Change Foundation, and the Saskatchewan Environment Corporation. According to the bill, these corporations will administer the cap-and-trade program and provide funding for research and public education.

Ontario. In 2009, the Ontario government passed Bill 185, which provides the government the authority to set up a greenhouse gas cap-and-trade system in Ontario. According to preliminary documents, the government is examining two kinds of caps: a 17 percent reduction from 2005 levels by 2020, with higher targets for the electric sector; or a 15 percent reduction from 2012 levels by 2020 (Ontario MOE 2009). Other elements of current proposals are modeled after existing systems, in particular the Waxman-Markey bill that passed the US House of Representatives in mid-2009. Further development of Ontario's cap-and-trade system has been suspended until after the October 2011 provincial elections, and its future depends heavily on whether the ruling Liberal Party retains power.[13]

---

11. Shawn McCarthy, "B.C., Ontario Hinder California Green Plan," *Globe and Mail*, April 13, 2011, www.theglobeandmail.com (accessed on May 6, 2011).

12. The baseline was not specified in the press release. See Government of Saskatchewan, "Saskatchewan Takes Real Action to Reduce Greenhouse Gas Emissions," May 11, 2009, www.gov.sk.ca (accessed on May 6, 2011).

13. Shawn McCarthy, "B.C., Ontario Hinder California Green Plan," *Globe and Mail*, April 13, 2011, www.theglobeandmail.com (accessed on May 6, 2011).

Manitoba. Bill 15, enacted in Manitoba in 2008, allows the lieutenant governor to make regulations "respecting the use of economic and financial instruments and market-based approaches" to achieve Manitoba's emissions reduction targets, including its WCI obligations.[14] The bill also authorizes new vehicle standards and requires Manitoba Hydro to refrain from using coal to generate electricity. In February 2011, Manitoba issued a short document explaining cap-and-trade to the public and soliciting comments (Manitoba Conservation 2011).

Clean Electricity

Renewable Standards

The renewable portfolio standard as a legislative mandate is somewhat less ubiquitous among provinces wishing to promote renewable energy than it is in the United States. Provinces have adopted other measures related to renewable energy in addition to the renewable portfolio standard, including provincial goals and performance standards. Three provinces have renewable portfolio standards. Under New Brunswick and Ontario regulations, 10 percent of electricity has had to come from renewable sources since 2010 (in Ontario, this renewable energy must be new), and Nova Scotia requires almost 20 percent of electricity to come from renewable sources by 2013.

Other provinces, meanwhile, have embraced nonbinding goals for the composition of renewable energy generated in province. Alberta has set a nonbinding provincial target that required it to generate 12.5 percent of electricity from renewable and alternative sources by 2008; this figure rises to 20 percent by 2020. Ontario aims to double hydropower, as well as wind, and solar power, by 2025. British Columbia has adopted a voluntary standard for utilities to achieve 10 percent of new generation from renewable sources. Though these targets are voluntary, most power generation in Canada is controlled by provincial monopolies. Generally, these firms are either responsible to provincial governments or are government owned. Opportunities for independent power producers exist in most provinces but are limited in scope. An exception is Alberta, whose market is deregulated (Blake, Cassels and Graydon, LLP 2008).

Several provinces have adopted electricity performance standards requiring facilities to eliminate coal and offset existing emissions. All coal-fired generation plants in Ontario are supposed to close by 2014. The coal-fired generation is being replaced with new renewable generation, and nuclear plants have been refurbished in order to maintain existing capacity.[15] New and replacement electrical generation facilities in Saskatchewan had to be carbon neutral—either greenhouse gas–free or fully offset by emissions credits—by 2007. In 2007,

---

14. Bill 15, Section 20(1)(f).

15. Tom Willatt and Sharon Saylor, "Canada's Provincial Power Strategies," *Power Magazine*, March 1, 2011, www.powermag.com (accessed on May 6, 2011).

British Columbia began requiring CCS for all coal-fired electricity generation facilities; this requirement effectively prevents any coal-fired plants from
being built in British Columbia, as carbon capture technology has not yet been
tested on a commercial scale. By 2016, electricity generation facilities in British
Columbia must also be carbon neutral. New Brunswick is moving forward
with new nuclear generation, with a new mid-sized reactor expected to be built
as part of a clean energy park.

Feed-In Tariffs

In 2006, Ontario became the first Canadian province to implement the
Standard Offer Program, which paid a constant price for renewable energy
generated within the province—11 cents per kilowatt hour (kWh) for wind,
biomass, and small hydropower, and 42 cents per kWh for solar power. The
electricity it could pay for was capped at 1,000 megawatt hours over 10 years.
This limit was exceeded in the first year of operation.

The Standard Offer Program was reintroduced in 2009 as a revamped
feed-in tariff (FIT), which provides a guaranteed stable price for renewable
energy over 20 years. The program includes most renewable sources, including
biomass, biogas, landfill gas, on-shore and off-shore wind, solar photovoltaic,
and run-of-the-river hydropower; it imposes a 50 megawatt (MW) limit. Tariffs
are designed to provide projects with an 11 percent return on equity and vary
according to source; landfill gas projects can earn 10 cents per kWh, whereas
small solar rooftop projects can reap as much as 80 cents per kWh (Powell
and Reid 2010). These subsidies are funded by rate payers, whose cost of electricity incorporates the cost of the FIT. As of September 2010, the program had
awarded 2,100 MW of contracts.

While Ontario's FIT has been enormously successful at generating new
renewable electricity, its design likely violates NAFTA and World Trade
Organization (WTO) rules. Subsidies are contingent upon a domestic content
requirement of 25 percent for wind turbines and 50 percent for solar panels.
Not surprisingly, this provision has been challenged in WTO dispute settlement by Japan, which requested formal bilateral consultations in September
2010.

British Columbia and Nova Scotia are currently developing their own
feed-in tariffs. Though both proposals subsidize in-province generation,
neither proposal contains an explicit domestic content requirement. Unlike
Ontario's FIT, which is aimed at increasing renewable energy use and
decreasing carbon emissions, British Columbia's program is targeted toward
emerging technologies. As British Columbia already derives 90 percent of its
electricity from hydropower, relatively mature renewable technologies such
as solar and wind are excluded from the feed-in tariff except in certain areas
that renewable electricity has not yet penetrated. British Columbia's program
aims to provide a 5 to 10 percent return on equity for developers (BCMEM
2010).

Nova Scotia's proposed feed-in tariff is expected to finance 100 MW of renewable energy, including small wind producers with a capacity of less than 50 kilowatts. Unlike British Columbia and Ontario, Nova Scotia requires projects to be community owned, whether by municipalities, universities, First Nation communities, nonprofits, or co-ops.[16] Eligible sources include wind, combined heat and power biomass facilities, small-scale in-stream tidal, and run-of-the-river hydropower (Nova Scotia DOE 2010).

Fuels

Ethanol Mandates

Although circumstances are changing—California recently released the final version of its low-carbon fuel standard, which regulates the carbon intensity of fuels in a comprehensive manner—the primary clean fuel policies used in North America are those designed to encourage production of ethanol and biodiesel. As in the United States, Canadian biofuels policy is engineered not only to promote biofuels as a lower-carbon, renewable source of energy, but also to support domestic agricultural producers. Provinces, too, tend to favor provincial agricultural interests. Support policies for biofuels include composition standards, subsidies, tax breaks, tariffs, nontariff barriers, and farm subsidies. In addition to the coordination problem posed by federal-provincial preemption, in the case of biofuel mandates and subsidies there is also the problem of inefficiencies caused by preferential treatment for provincial interests.

Seven Canadian provinces have ethanol composition standards: Alberta, British Columbia, New Brunswick, Ontario, Québec, Saskatchewan, and Manitoba. Québec is the only province that has a composition standard solely for cellulosic ethanol—5 percent by 2012. Of the six with more-general ethanol standards, Manitoba's standard, which requires 8.5 percent average ethanol composition as of 2008, is the most stringent.[17] Total annual subsidies to ethanol producers from both the federal and provincial governments will total almost C$2 billion between 2007 and 2012, excluding biodiesel and second-generation ethanol grants (Auld 2008).

These ethanol programs often lead to unintended drawbacks. Larger incentives for smaller facilities and agricultural producers reduce economies of scale. Farm support programs for producers of corn for ethanol also raise grain prices, adversely impacting livestock growers and the general public. While these costs are spread out across Canada (and elsewhere; higher food prices due to ethanol subsidies have also adversely impacted developing countries), benefits are concentrated in the three provinces that account for the vast majority of Canada's corn crop: Ontario, Québec, and Manitoba. Douglas Auld (2008) esti-

---

16. The exception is in-stream tidal, which faces no limits on ownership.

17. Previously, Manitoba had a standard requiring 85 percent of gasoline to contain 10 percent ethanol by 2005, but this was never enforced due to lack of capacity.

mates that the total wealth transfers to farmers in these provinces amounted to C$600 million in 2008 and will amount to C$800 million in 2012.

Ethanol policies use tariffs and nontariff barriers to promote domestic production or production in province. Most imported biofuels come from the United States, which has tariff-free access to the Canadian market under NAFTA; Canada levies a small tariff on some imported biofuels from other countries. Most-favored nation (MFN) tariffs on biofuels were 6.5 percent as of January 2009, and the General Preferential Tariff was 3 percent.[18] A 2008 shift from excise tax reductions to production tax credits for biofuels at both the federal and provincial levels has reduced support for biofuels manufactured outside of Canada and provided an advantage to biofuels produced domestically. British Columbia, Manitoba, Saskatchewan, and Québec explicitly favor ethanol produced in the province with feedstocks produced in the province when offering provincial support to producers (Fox and Shwedel 2007). For example, Husky Energy agreed that 80 percent of feedstock needed for its wheat-based facility in Manitoba will be supplied by Manitoba producers (Laan, Litman, and Steenblik 2009).

The tide of scientific opinion on the environmental merits of the type of biofuels produced in Canada has shifted in recent years, however. Timothy Searchinger (2008) argues that corn-based ethanol's emissions were underestimated, since the existing models assume that all corn is grown on land with no preexisting vegetation. If this assumption were true, growing corn would provide a significant sequestration benefit. In fact, however, corn grown for ethanol production displaces existing vegetation; as a result, emissions from ethanol actually exceed those from gasoline. Indeed, Nobel laureate Paul Crutzen warns that corn ethanol could produce 50 percent more emissions than gasoline when NO_2 emissions from fertilizer are taken into account (Crutzen et al. 2008).

There are indications that Canadian federal and local governments are beginning to transition away from regulations promoting biofuels as a monolithic goal to regulations based on the carbon content of fuels over their life cycle, from the cultivation of feedstocks to the refining stage to the combustion of the fuels. The federal government published a notice of intent in 2006 regarding the Canadian national renewable fuels mandate, which acknowledged the questionability of environmental gains from grain ethanol (Environment Canada 2006).

Low-Carbon Fuel Standards

Ontario has committed to adopting California's low-carbon fuel standard, which will reduce the carbon intensity of passenger vehicle fuels by 10 percent by 2020, and British Columbia has a low-carbon fuel standard in place. British

---

18. Canada's MFN tariff amounts to about 10 cents per liter. By contrast, US biofuels tariffs amount to 54 cents per gallon.

Columbia's standard differs substantially from California's standard (described in chapter 2). Unlike California, British Columbia counts all crude oil as having equal carbon intensity; the regulation does not distinguish between oil sands and conventional crude. This decision will sharply lessen the potential impact of British Columbia's LCFS on the Albertan oil sands industry.

Interregional Harmonization Issues

The economic effects of climate legislation are likely to vary by province, even though the magnitude of these effects is under debate. Alberta has experienced the most emissions growth in absolute terms over the past 20 years, though Saskatchewan, Ontario, and British Columbia have also contributed significantly to Canada's increase in emissions (table 3.1; figure 3.1). The largest contributors to the problem are likely to experience the most dislocation going forward. Alberta's economy, in particular, is likely to experience the greatest changes from business-as-usual growth under a low-carbon regime. This is in part due to Alberta's heavy reliance on oil and gas extraction, and oil sands production in particular.

Regional differences in sources of electricity generation further sharpen the east-west provincial split. Alberta, Saskatchewan, and Nova Scotia are disproportionately dependent on coal-fired electricity generation. Table 3.2 shows that Alberta derives only 5 percent of electricity from renewable sources, and Nova Scotia only 8 percent. Alberta generates almost three-quarters of its electricity from coal; Saskatchewan and Nova Scotia generate about 60 percent from coal. In contrast, Newfoundland and Labrador, Québec, Manitoba, British Columbia, and the Yukon derive more than 90 percent of the electricity generated in province from renewable sources.[19] As a result, Albertan electricity generation produces over a hundred times as much GHG as British Columbian generation—almost 16 tons per capita.[20] Alberta has substantial potential for renewable energy in province, but it would need to quickly develop its renewable potential to meet GHG emissions targets under a new climate change regime.

Alberta is also highly dependent on carbon-intensive oil and gas extraction. The oil and gas industry provided the Albertan provincial government with over 15 percent of its revenues in the 2009–10 fiscal year (Government of Alberta 2010). Most of these revenues come from the oil sands. Alberta produced 1.3 million barrels per day of oil sands crude in 2009, which amounted to 70 percent of total Albertan crude production and about 50 percent of total Canadian production (EIA 2011b, Statistics Canada 2010a); see table 3.3. IHS CERA (2011) predicts that oil sands production will double in the next

19. Prince Edward Island is close behind, with 89 percent of its in-province electricity generated from wind and tidal sources.

20. Calculations are based on emissions data found at Environment Canada (2008b) and population data found at Statistics Canada (2010b).

Table 3.1 Greenhouse gas emissions by province and territory, 1990–2008
(million metric tons of CO_2 equivalent)

Province/territory	1990	1995	2000	2005	2008	Share of 2008 total (percent)	Change, 1990–2008 (percent)
Alberta	170	198	224	233	244	33.3	43.7
Ontario	175	175	201	201	190	25.9	8.7
Québec	85	83	86	89	82	11.2	–3.8
Saskatchewan	44	59	66	71	75	10.2	70.1
British Columbia	51	59	63	66	65	8.9	28.6
Manitoba	18	19	20	20	22	3.0	21.7
Nova Scotia	20	19	21	23	21	2.8	7.1
New Brunswick	16	17	20	21	18	2.4	10.9
Newfoundland and Labrador	10	9	9	11	10	1.4	2.0
Yukon, Northwest Territories, Nunavut (combined)	2	3	2	2	2	0.3	2.8
Prince Edward Island	2	2	2	2	2	0.3	–6.4
Canada	596	646	721	747	734	100	23.2

Note: Percentages are rounded and may not sum exactly to 100.

Source: Environment Canada (2010).

Figure 3.1 Greenhouse gas emissions in Canadian provinces, 1990–2005

millions of tons

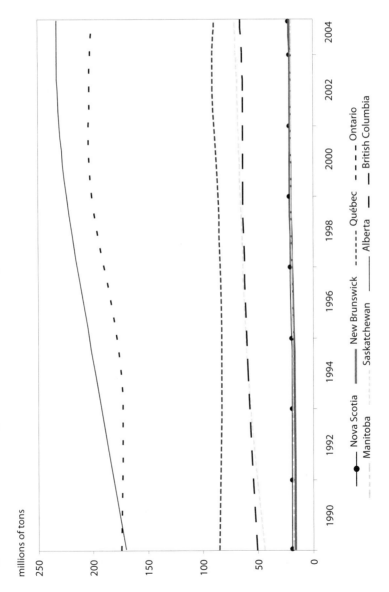

Source: Environment Canada (2008b).

Table 3.2 Electricity generation by source, 2007 (percent of total provincial megawatt hours)

Province	Hydro	Wind/tidal	Coal	Petroleum	Natural gas	Wood	Uranium	Other
Canada	59	1	17	1	7	0	15	1
Alberta	4	1	74	0	21	1	0	0
British Columbia	95	0	0	0	4	1	0	0
Manitoba	98	1	1	0	0	0	0	0
New Brunswick	17	0	18	24	11	0	25	5
Newfoundland and Labrador	97	0	0	3	0	0	0	0
Northwest Territories	75	0	0	12	13	0	0	0
Nova Scotia	7	1	57	7	6	1	0	20
Nunavut	0	0	0	100	0	0	0	0
Ontario	22	0	18	0	8	0	51	0
Prince Edward Island	0	89	0	3	0	8	0	0
Québec	94	0	0	0	3	0	2	0
Saskatchewan	22	3	61	0	14	0	0	0
Yukon	93	0	0	7	0	0	0	0

Note: Percentages are rounded and may not sum exactly to 100.

Source: Authors' calculations based on data from Statistics Canada (2009).

Table 3.3   Canadian crude oil production by province and type, 2009
(barrels per day)

Province	Light/medium, condensate, and pentanes plus	Heavy	Synthetic and crude bitumen	Total
Alberta	462	145	1,339	1,946
Saskatchewan	135	289	0	424
Newfoundland/Labrador	268	0	0	268
British Columbia	33	0	0	33
Manitoba	26	0	0	26
Northwest Territories	17	0	0	17
Nova Scotia	8	0	0	8
Ontario	2	0	0	2
Canada	951	434	1,339	2,724

Note: Provinces with negligible oil production are omitted.

Source: Authors' calculations using a conversion factor of 6.289 barrels per cubic meter, and data from Statistics Canada (2010a).

decade and grow to 3.1 million barrels per day by 2030. However, rosy fore-casts in the past of huge increases in oil production have run up against supply constraints and mounting environmental concerns.

Under business-as-usual scenarios, growth of oil sands is expected to continue to be one of the biggest drivers of greenhouse gas emissions in Canada. Oil sands production generates 5 to 15 percent more GHG on a well-to-wheel basis than the average basket of crude consumed in North America (IHS CERA 2010). It is not clear whether the oil sands' carbon footprint can be sufficiently reduced in the near term in a cost-effective manner. CCS, which could lower the oil sands' footprint to that of conventional petroleum, is unlikely to be cost-competitive with other means of reducing greenhouse gas emissions in the short run. McKinsey and Company (2008) estimates that CCS costs will range from about $80 to $115 per ton of CO_2 for early projects, possibly falling to $40 to $60 by 2030.[21] The RAND Corporation estimates CCS costs to range from $3.71 to $7.88 per barrel for mining projects and $5.67 to $10.80 for in situ production in the short run, dropping to $2.86 to $6.39 for mining and $4.36 to $8.73 for in situ production by 2025 (Toman et al. 2008). These numbers would seem to indicate that, absent significant technological improvements, a mandate to reduce greenhouse gas emissions is likely to impede the growth of the oil sands industry or greatly increase compliance costs.

---

21. These amounts and those elsewhere in the chapter are in US dollars unless Canadian dollars are specified.

Cost Estimates of GHG Reductions

The National Roundtable on the Environment and the Economy (NRTEE) finds that meeting Canada's Copenhagen target would retard GDP growth by 0.2 percent, producing a 2 percent loss in GDP in 2020 relative to business-as-usual levels. This translates into a household welfare loss of 0.5 percent relative to business-as-usual levels. Total GDP growth between 2010 and 2020 is predicted to be 23 percent under the reference case scenario and 21 percent under the Copenhagen target scenario (NRTEE 2011; see also table 3.4).

According to the model used by the NRTEE, however, the relatively modest cost of a national program belies significant regional differences. The study foresees a 4.5 percent GDP decline in 2020 relative to the reference case in Alberta, and a 2.8 percent decline in Saskatchewan. In terms of growth rates, the NRTEE predicts 2.1 percent GDP growth in Alberta per year under business as usual and 1.8 percent growth if Canada achieves its Copenhagen target. The smallest GDP decline is in Manitoba, which experiences a loss in GDP growth of 0.1 percent and a cumulative GDP loss of 1 percent in 2020 (NRTEE 2011).

A report sponsored by the Pembina Institute and the David Suzuki Foundation predicts even more drastic differences among the provinces. It calculates that if Alberta met government targets it would lose 7.3 to 8.5 percent of GDP between 2010 and 2020 relative to the business-as-usual case; on the other hand, the GDP of Manitoba, which obtains almost all of its electricity from hydropower and does not have significant carbon-intensive manufacturing, would increase 1.9 to 2.1 percent relative to the business-as-usual case (Bataille et al. 2009).[22]

As in the United States, appropriate policy responses can alleviate inequalities among different locales. Jotham Peters et al. (2010) find that a transfer of revenues back to the provinces, for the purpose of lowering personal and corporate income taxes, can reduce adverse GDP impacts in Alberta and Saskatchewan by one-third, relative to a cap-and-trade system that distributes revenues on an even per capita basis throughout Canada. The NRTEE (2011) study reaches a similar conclusion; with free output-based allocations on an emissions intensity benchmark, the adverse GDP impact of climate policy on Alberta is reduced from 4.5 to 1.6 percent.

Canadian Policy and US Legislation

In climate change, as in many other areas, Canadian policymakers need to keep a watchful eye on developments south of the border. Going forward, Canada has several unhappy options. It could wait for the United States to act and then emulate it when it does. Or it could go it alone while it waits for the United States to sort out the political issues that have delayed decisions on climate

---

22. The Pembina-Suzuki report, however, has been criticized for assuming a fixed aggregate capital stock. See Jack Mintz, "Our Costly Climate Plan," *National Post*, December 10, 2009.

Table 3.4 Cost estimates of reducing greenhouse gas emissions in Canada

Source	Scenario	2020 targets	Estimated effect (percent of GDP relative to business as usual)						
			Canada	Alberta	British Columbia	Manitoba	Québec	Ontario	Saskatchewan
National Roundtable on the Environment and the Economy (NRTEE 2011)	Canada leads, no US action	17 percent below 2005 levels	−2.0	−4.5	−2.5	−1.0	−1.4	−1.2	−2.8
	Canada harmonizes with the United States on targets	17 percent below 2005 levels	−2.3	−4.7	−3.3	−1.3	−1.7	−1.5	−3.1
	OECD acts together	25 percent below 1990 levels	−3.0	−11.9	−4.2	2.7	−1.3	0	−4.7
	OECD acts together	20 percent below 2006 levels	−1.4	−7.3	−2.2	1.9	−0.7	0.6	−1.2
Bataille et al. (2009)	Canada goes further than OECD	25 percent below 1990 levels	−3.2	−12.1	−4.8	2.1	−1.3	0	−7.5
	Canada goes further than OECD	20 percent below 2006 levels	−1.5	−8.5	−2.5	2.1	−0.3	0.9	−2.8

OECD = Organization for Economic Cooperation and Development

Sources: NRTEE (2011); Bataille et al. (2009).

change policy. If it adopts the second approach, it must then choose whether to adapt its policies to those of its neighbor once the United States implements a climate change regime, or continue its original policies regardless of what the United States does. All of these options have advantages and drawbacks.

Below, we discuss three possibilities for Canada: the United States acts and Canada does not; both the United States and Canada act; and Canada acts and the United States does not. In the first and last scenarios, Canada's energy-intensive industries could face competitiveness impacts, depending on how policies are managed. The second scenario, coordinated action with the United States, would be the best scenario for Canada, but given US regulatory uncertainty, Canada will likely need to develop an alternate strategy.

Border Allowance Program: If the United States Acts and Canada Does Not

The US border allowance program is as yet deferred to some future date. US climate legislation has been put on the back burner, and even if Congress had acted, the international reserve allowance program in the Waxman-Markey bill was not scheduled to begin until 2020 and the similar program in the Kerry-Lieberman bill not until 2025 or later. Benjamin Dachis (2009) calculates that 89 percent of Canadian trade with the United States would have been exempted under the Waxman-Markey bill due to its low carbon intensity, but the pulp and paper sector would be vulnerable. Employment in this industry is concentrated in a handful of provinces. In addition, low-carbon fuel standards and other regulations in the United States could directly affect Canada's petroleum sector (see chapter 2 for a more detailed explanation of this point).

Canadian officials understand these vulnerabilities and have sought to address them by promising to model efforts on climate change after those of the United States. The targets that Canada put forth in Copenhagen were explicitly tied to actions taken by the United States; and while cap-and-trade was being discussed in the United States, Prime Minister Stephen Harper repeatedly promised to work with the United States to harmonize legislation in order to avoid the imposition of border measures.[23] So long as Canadian legislation conforms to that of the United States, Canada should be able to avoid prospective imposition of border measures against its energy-intensive exports to the United States.

Both the Waxman-Markey bill in the House of Representatives and the Kerry-Boxer bill in the Senate included international reserve allowance programs; these programs require importers of trade-intensive, carbon-intensive products to buy allowances at the border to compensate for the difference between the cost of producing energy-intensive manufactures in the United

---

23. See UNFCCC (2010b); see also Kate Galbraith, "Harper on US-Canada Energy Relations," *New York Times Green Blog*, September 18, 2009, http://green.blogs.nytimes.com (accessed on May 6, 2011).

States and the cost in countries that do not adopt climate measures as stringent as the United States'. A border allowance program would be economically equivalent to a tariff on qualifying imports.

Countries wishing to avoid the border adjustment program must have done one of three things:

1. entered into an international agreement that includes a nationally enforceable economy-wide national emissions reduction target at least as stringent as that of the United States;
2. entered into a sectoral agreement with the United States; or
3. achieved a greenhouse gas intensity for the sector in question that is less than or equal to that of the United States.

In order to secure its position as a compliant country for all sectors, therefore, Canada would need to adopt a greenhouse gas reduction program that achieves comparable reductions to the program adopted in the United States.

If the United States adopts a cap-and-trade program in the next decade, both the intensity targets and technology fund proposed in Canadian legislation could expose Canada to the threat of a US international reserve allowance program if these provisions preclude Canada from complying with its commitments under an international treaty or from making commitments as stringent as those of the United States. Depending on the price per ton of CO_2e set for the technology fund, the fund could cause Canada's program to work more like a carbon tax, which establishes price certainty, than a cap-and-trade program, which establishes certainty regarding the level of emissions reductions. Even if Canada established a carbon price equivalent to that of the United States through the technology fund, an equivalent price is not likely to translate into an equivalent percentage reduction below 2005 levels, given Canada's higher predicted emissions growth under business as usual. Insofar as it prevents Canada from achieving a carbon reduction program equivalent to that of the United States, the technology fund provision could make Canada vulnerable to US border adjustments under various climate change regimes recently considered by the US Congress.

There are several reasons why it is unlikely that Canada would be subject to border measures in practice, however. First and foremost, as a defensive measure against this provision, the Canadian government has pledged to align its emissions targets with those of the United States and to closely follow US climate change policies. None of the US competitiveness measures proposed to date has required foreign countries to conform every detail of their regulations to US law; rather, the measures have simply required that emissions reductions resulting from foreign regulation be comparable. So long as Canada adopts the same emissions reduction commitments in international negotiations as the United States does and is able to follow through on its commitments, it is highly unlikely that border measures would apply.

Second, recent US legislative proposals have given the government the discretion to suspend border allowance measures if they pose a significant risk to the US economy. In the Waxman-Markey bill, this requires a joint resolution from Congress; in the Kerry-Lieberman bill, discretion is left up to the president. Given Canada's importance as a supplier of carbon-intensive manufactures to the United States, and keeping in mind that these manufactures tend to be intermediate goods upon which US industries rely, one would expect Canadian sectors to be exempted from the border allowance provision in the event that the program is initially determined to apply to Canada.

Third, the application of the program is likely to be suspended for at least a decade, giving Canadian officials plenty of time to consult with US officials to harmonize aspects of their respective programs that might prove problematic. The international reserve allowance program was put off until 2020 in the Waxman-Markey bill and 2025 or beyond in the Kerry-Lieberman bill. Moreover, the international reserve allowance program would likely be administered by the EPA, allowing presidential administrations to use their discretion to prevent protectionism.

It is important to reiterate that the Kerry-Lieberman bill and the final version of the Waxman-Markey bill exempted sectors with a carbon intensity less than or equal to that in the United States. For the sake of thoroughness, we detail the potential impacts on Canadian exports under a prospective US program that omits the sectoral intensity exception.

With the intensity exemption, only the pulp and paper sector would be affected (Dachis 2009). Vulnerable paper and wood product exports total about $10 billion (table 3.5). The paper mill product sector is among the sectors most in competition between the two countries; these exports total $2.3 billion (table 3.5). Table 3.6 shows the concentration of employment in carbon-intensive industries by province.[24] The pulp, paper, and paperboard industries account for 6.9 percent in New Brunswick, 5.6 percent in British Columbia, and 3.6 percent in Québec.

Table 3.5 lists the products, at the six-digit NAICS level, that would have qualified for rebates by the United States under the Waxman-Markey bill. Without the intensity exception, all of these products could be eligible for border adjustments if neither of the other two conditions above is met. These industries total $47 billion in exports (table 3.5). British Columbia and Québec share the highest burden in terms of employment at risk; they have over 11 percent of manufacturing employment in industries that would be eligible for the international reserve allowance program under the Waxman-Markey bill and that export more than $200 million annually to the United States. Alberta and New Brunswick are close behind, with almost 10 percent of manufacturing employment in these sectors. Ontario has almost 7 percent of manufacturing employment in these sectors (table 3.6).

What would be the likely effect of border measures if implemented against

---

24. Due to lack of data, our estimates of employment numbers are likely to underestimate actual levels.

Table 3.5 Trade-vulnerable industries and US trade with Canada, 2008[a]

NAICS code/category	Description	US imports from Canada (millions of US dollars)[b]	US exports to Canada (millions of US dollars)[c]	Index of intra-industry traded
Food products				
311221	**Wet corn milling products**	**188**	**280**	**0.80**
31131X	Sugars	37	46	0.89
Paper and wood products				
321219	Reconstituted wood products	1,051	254	0.39
322110	Pulp mill products	2,867	132	0.09
322121	**Paper (except newsprint) mill products**	**2,345**	**1,518**	**0.79**
322122	Newsprint mill products	4,849	127	0.05
322130	Paperboard mill products	122	1	0.02
Chemicals				
314992	Tire cords and tire fabrics	98	57	0.74
325110	**Petrochemicals**	**2,213**	**739**	**0.50**
325131	**Inorganic dyes and pigments**	**290**	**260**	**0.95**
325132	Synthetic organic dyes and pigments	19	86	0.36
325181	**Alkalies and chlorine**	**152**	**201**	**0.86**
325182	Carbon black	123	94	0.87
325188	**All other basic inorganic chemicals**	**1,976**	**948**	**0.65**
325191	Gum and wood chemicals	11	31	0.52
325192	Cyclic crude and intermediates	1,286	240	0.31

Code	Description			
325193	Ethyl alcohols	35	308	0.20
325199	**All other basic organic chemicals**	**1,440**	**3,318**	**0.61**
325211	**Plastics materials and resins**	**5,218**	**5,063**	**0.98**
325212	**Synthetic rubbers**	**243**	**621**	**0.56**
325222	**Noncellulosic organic fibers**	**303**	**310**	**0.99**
325311	Nitrogenous fertilizers	1,940	154	0.15
335991	**Carbon and graphite products**	**75**	**214**	**0.52**
Nonmetallic mineral products				
327111	China plumbing fixtures and china and earthenware bathroom accessories	0	51	0
327112	China, fine earthenware, and other pottery products	5	153	0.06
327113	Porcelain electrical supplies	28	26	0.96
327122	Ceramic wall and floor tiles	2	24	0.15
327123	Other structural ceramic products	0	2	0
327124	Clay and alumina articles	20	30	0.80
327125	Nonclay refractory articles	71	123	0.73
327211	**Drawn, blown, float, and flat glass**	**155**	**379**	**0.58**
327212	**Other pressed and blown glass and glassware**	**162**	**332**	**0.66**

(continued on next page)

Table 3.5 Trade-vulnerable industries and US trade with Canada, 2008[a] *(continued)*

NAICS code/ category	Description	US imports from Canada (millions of US dollars)[b]	US exports to Canada (millions of US dollars)[c]	Index of intra-industry traded
Nonmetallic mineral products				
327213	Glass containers	131	177	0.85
327310	Cements	338	84	0.40
327410	Lime and calcined dolomite	32	23	0.84
327992	Ground or treated mineral and earth	48	52	0.96
327993	**Mineral wool and glass fibers**	**208**	**248**	**0.91**
Ferrous metals				
331111	**Iron and steel**	**6,847**	**7,182**	**0.98**
331112	Electrometallurgical ferro-alloy product	123	111	0.95
Nonferrous metals				
331311	Alumina refining	12	239	0.10
331312	Primary aluminum	5,527	313	0.11
331419	Primary smelting and refining of nonferrous metals (except copper and aluminum)	6,396	793	0.22
Total		46,986	25,344	n.a.

NAICS = North American Industry Classification System; n.a. = not applicable

a. Sectors in bold meet two criteria: The index of intra-industry trade has a value of 0.5 or larger; and either exports or imports exceed $200 million annually (based on 2008 figures).

b. This column includes imports for consumption: foreign goods that immediately enter US consumption channels. Goods being held in bonded warehouses or US foreign trade zones are not included until they are withdrawn for consumption.

c. This column includes domestic exports: goods that are grown, mined, produced, or manufactured in the United States and sent to foreign countries. Domestic exports include goods from US foreign trade zones that have been enhanced in value.

d. The index of intra-industry trade is calculated using the formula $[1 - |X - M|/(X + M)]$, where X = US exports to Canada (fourth column) and M = US imports from Canada (third column).

Source: Hufbauer and Kim (2009).

Table 3.6   Number of people employed in carbon-intensive industries, by province, 2008

NAICS code/sector	Nova Scotia	New Brunswick	Québec	Ontario	Manitoba	Saskatchewan	Alberta	British Columbia
3221: Pulp, paper, and paperboard mills	C	2,137	15,663	7,632	C	n.a.	2,375	8,883
3212: Veneer, plywood, and engineered wood product manufacturing	505	578	5,938	5,079	505	712	2,752	5,703
3273: Cement and concrete product manufacturing	C	n.a.	6,769	10,683	944	C	3,592	3,099
3279: Other nonmetallic mineral product manufacturing	C	360	2,753	4,185	135	n.a.	C	C
3253: Pesticide, fertilizer, and other agricultural chemical manufacturing	n.a.	C	n.a.	C	n.a.	C	1,565	n.a.
3251: Basic chemical manufacturing	n.a.	n.a.	2,943	6,612	C	n.a.	3,313	470
3252: Resin, synthetic rubber, and artificial and synthetic fibers and filaments manufacturing	n.a.	n.a.	C	C	n.a.	n.a.	n.a.	n.a.
3311: Iron and steel mills and ferro-alloy manufacturing	n.a.	n.a.	2,229	14,777	n.a.	n.a.	n.a.	n.a.
3313: Alumina and aluminum production and processing	n.a.	n.a.	11,024	C	n.a.	n.a.	n.a.	n.a.
3314: Nonferrous metal (except aluminum) production and processing	n.a.	n.a.	3,326	C	n.a.	n.a.	n.a.	n.a.

(continued on next page)

Table 3.6 Number of people employed in carbon-intensive industries, by province, 2008 *(continued)*

NAICS code/sector	Nova Scotia	New Brunswick	Québec	Ontario	Manitoba	Saskatchewan	Alberta	British Columbia
Total	505	3,075	50,645	48,968	1,584	712	13,597	18,155
Percent of total manufacturing employment	1.5	9.9	11.2	6.5	2.6	2.6	9.9	11.5
Percent of total employment	0.1	1	1.5	0.9	0.3	0.2	0.8	1

NAICS = North American Industry Classification System

n.a. = not applicable; contains too few employees to appear in Statistics Canada tables.

C = data suppressed by Statistics Canada to meet the confidentiality requirements of the Statistics Act.

Note: Due to lack of data, our estimates of employment numbers are likely to underestimate actual levels.

Source: Statistics Canada, "Employment by enterprise size of employment (SEPH) for all employees, unadjusted for seasonal variation, for selected industries classified using the North American Industry Classification System (NAICS), annually," www.statcan.gc.ca (accessed on June 4, 2009).

Canadian industries? Neither the Senate nor the House bill specifies the methodology for calculating the number of allowances importers would need to purchase at the border under the program; rather, these details are left up to the EPA. Thus, it is difficult to say how Canadian imports would be treated in practice. A major variable would be whether the cost of climate-related performance standards, provincial cap-and-trade programs and regulations, and the like would be taken into account in determining the allowance burden for importers.

Cross-Border Allowance Trading: If Both Countries Act

It will probably cost more for Canada to achieve the same GHG emissions reductions as the United States. The US Energy Information Administration (EIA) projects that Canada's carbon dioxide emissions will grow at 0.3 percent per year between 2006 and 2030 under business-as-usual conditions. In contrast, US emissions are projected to grow by only 0.2 percent per year. Canada is also projected to have a higher carbon dioxide intensity in 2035 under business as usual: almost 300 metric tons per million dollars of GDP. US carbon dioxide intensity in 2030 is projected to be 250 metric tons per million dollars of GDP (EIA 2010). The difference in projected GHG emissions growth is largely due to the projected growth of emissions from Alberta's oil sands (NRTEE 2011).[25]

In order to achieve the same carbon-intensity and absolute carbon reductions as the United States, Canada must make greater reductions from business-as-usual levels. Sawyer and Fischer (2010) estimate that absent allowance trading, the cost of emissions allowances in Canada will be substantially greater to achieve the same quantity of carbon emissions reductions; the cost will be twice as much as in the United States if Canada harmonizes its program completely with US proposals. Likewise, NRTEE (2011) estimates that if Canada and the United States harmonize on a 17 percent emissions reduction target, carbon prices will reach $54 per ton in the United States and $78 per ton in Canada. Because the United States' GHG output is ten times that of Canada, its carbon market will determine the overall US-Canada allowance price if Canada links to it. As a result, allowance trading with the United States could alleviate cost pressures for energy-intensive industries, particularly for exports.

Allowance trading could have substantial benefits for energy-intensive industries and overall GDP. If Canada is able to retain the policy framework set out in Turning the Corner and is also able to trade allowances with the United States, adverse GDP impacts could be reduced by almost 50 percent, and adverse impacts on exports could be reduced sixfold (Sawyer and Fischer 2010). Sectoral impacts on oil, gas, mining, and manufacturing could also be reduced significantly.

Complete harmonization with a US climate program would also ensure

25. IHS CERA (2011) projects that the oil sands share of total Canadian emissions will grow from 5 percent in 2010 to 10 percent in 2030.

that Canada would not be subject to climate-related trade measures from the United States. As we argued earlier, Canada will likely be safe from border measures so long as its program is able to reduce emissions as much as the US program.

If a future US program were similar to the Waxman-Markey and Kerry-Lieberman bills, harmonization could have disadvantages for Canada (Sawyer and Fischer 2010). Canada would need to have an absolute, mandatory emissions limit and would need to have provisions comparable to those of the United States on a number of issues—including monitoring, compliance, quality of offsets, and restrictions on the use of offsets—in order to trade allowances with the United States (see chapter 2). The intensity-based cap espoused by Canada's Turning the Corner plan would almost certainly violate this condition.[26]

Canada's proposed offset system might also pose an issue. Canada's most recently proposed offset plan allows unlimited use of domestic offsets, although international certified emissions reductions under the UN Framework Convention on Climate Change are limited to 10 percent of a firm's compliance obligation. In contrast, the Waxman-Markey bill restricted total offset use to 27 to 32 percent of compliance obligation for firms between 2012 and 2025; it set ceilings on total economy-wide offsets at 2 billion tons and on international offsets at 1 billion tons. In sum, Canada adopts a somewhat stricter approach to international offset use but a far more lenient approach to domestic offset use. In order to trade allowances with the United States, Canada would need to alter these provisions in accordance with the US model.[27]

Still, there are other drawbacks to carbon market linkage. As a net buyer of US allowances, Canada would experience large financial outflows to the United States (Sawyer and Fischer 2010). In addition, the lower allowance price in Canada could lessen incentives for development and deployment of new technologies, particularly CCS, which could increase the cost of reducing emissions later on. Given Canadian politics to date, however, we think it likely that the Canadian government would find the benefits of linking carbon markets—reduction of costs for carbon-intensive industries and alleviation of the impacts on exports—to be worth these costs.

---

26. Still, this deviation from Turning the Corner might not be a significant barrier for Canada. At the time the Waxman-Markey and Kerry-Lieberman bills were being debated in the United States, Canadian officials emphasized policy alignment with the United States—including an alignment of targets—over a commitment to the specifics of the Turning the Corner proposal. See, for example, the speech by Jim Prentice to the North American Forum of the Canadian Council of Chief Executives, Ottawa, October 6, 2009.

27. Nevertheless, allowance trading with the United States might not require Canada to implement a higher-cost climate regime. Sawyer and Fischer (2010) argue that costs would rise under a harmonized scenario primarily due to coverage of the building and transportation sectors, which were not regulated under the Turning the Corner plan. Even if Canada omits these sectors, it could still trade allowances with the United States according to recent US climate change bills considered.

Going It Alone: If Canada Acts and the United States Does Not

Given the unfavorable congressional response to the 2009 US climate legislation, it will likely be years before the United States again considers implementing a cap-and-trade program. In any case, international emissions trading has been a low priority for US politicians thus far. If Canada waits for the opportunity to trade allowances with the United States before implementing its own program, its own climate change regime could be put on hold indefinitely. Such delay could increase the long-term cost to Canada of reducing emissions.

As a consequence of this uncertainty—and keeping in mind that harmonization with the United States would entail costs as well as benefits—Canada may be best advised to go it alone for now, and perhaps attempt to link its market or its allowance price to that of the United States once a carbon price is in place south of the border. The NRTEE suggests that Canada adopt a C\$30 carbon price collar that limits Canada's carbon price to no more than C\$30 per ton more than the US price. In other words, if the United States continues to stall on carbon pricing, Canada's carbon price would be limited to C\$30 per ton. If the United States adopts carbon-pricing legislation such as a cap-and-trade system, however, Canada's price could rise. This price collar allows Canada to take early action on climate change while limiting competitiveness impacts for its manufacturing and energy industries. In addition, such a transitional program would limit the risk that Canada would be subject to border measures if the United States were to pass a cap-and-trade bill similar to recent congressional proposals (NRTEE 2011).

The Oil Sands

Chapter 2 describes a number of other US policies that could have spillover effects on Canada. Among the most notable from Canada's perspective are policies that US states and the Obama administration have adopted toward the oil sands. Canada is the leading supplier of oil to the US market: US imports of Canadian crude oil and refined products in 2008 totaled 2.5 million barrels per day out of a total Canadian production of 3.4 million barrels per day (EIA 2011b). Canadian oil sands syncrudes are expected to continue to be an important energy source for the US market: The US Energy Information Administration predicts that oil sands production, along with increased biofuel supplies, will account for 70 percent of the projected incremental US supply between 2009 and 2035 (EIA 2011a).

The GHG output of oil sands mining is considerably more than that of conventional oil drilling, and Canadian firms have a stake in whether and how US environmental regulatory agencies account for this carbon impact. Low-carbon fuel standards, if widely adopted, could constrain US imports of oil sands crude (see chapter 2). Another issue is whether the United States approves the Keystone XL pipeline, which is expected to transport oil from

Canada to the Gulf Coast. An initial State Department environmental impact assessment was challenged by the EPA, which argued that the assessment did not take into account the additional GHG emissions resulting from an expansion of oil sands output and failed to consider new fuel efficiency regulations when determining whether the pipeline was necessary for energy security. Additional objections have arisen to its proposed location through the Ogallala Aquifer, which supplies 80 percent of Nebraska's drinking water.[28]

As a result of the controversy, the State Department has delayed the decision regarding approval until the end of 2011. In the meantime, it issued a Supplementary Draft Environmental Impact Statement in April 2011 in order to address environmental concerns, but stressed that the additional document does not alter its conclusions as to the pipeline's benefits (US Department of State 2011). The EPA has maintained that the supplemental statement does not sufficiently address environmental impacts.[29]

The controversy introduces some uncertainty into the US market. While the US market is integral to the development of Canadian oil resources, Canada is attempting to branch out to other customers. Even if an LCFS is implemented throughout North America, the Asian market is likely to remain unregulated and an anxious trading partner. Although Canada is dependent on the US market for its oil sands exports, it is starting to build infrastructure for oil exports to Asia. Enbridge, Inc., a Canadian energy company, has proposed a pipeline to carry up to 900,000 barrels per day to a port at Kitimat, from which oil could be transported overseas in tankers. China's energy firm Sinopec bought a 9 percent stake in Syncrude Canada Ltd. in April 2010, a development that could accelerate the construction of this pipeline.[30] In addition, Kinder Morgan Canada has proposed an expansion of an existing pipeline to carry 700,000 barrels per day to the Port of Vancouver. With these two pipelines in place, up to 1.6 million barrels per day could be shipped abroad, providing another market in case US states adopt a low-carbon fuel standard.[31] However, the projects remain speculative at this stage, particularly construction of the Kinder Morgan pipeline, and regulatory approval and construction would delay the projects at least until the end of the decade. As a result, exports to Asia are not a near-term option.

---

28. Lee-Anne Goodman, "US Set to Approve Keystone XL Pipeline," *Globe and Mail*, October 20, 2010.

29. Cynthia Giles, Assistant Administrator for the Office of Enforcement and Compliance Assurance, to Jose W. Fernandez and Kerri-Ann Jones, June 6, 2011, www.eenews.net (accessed on June 10, 2011).

30. Shawn McCarthy, "China's Big Move into Alberta," *Globe and Mail*, April 13, 2010, B01.

31. See Duke Du Plessis and Nancy Wu, "Marketability of Oil Sands Products in Asian Countries," presentation to the Hydrocarbon Updating Task Force, June 20, 2007, www.energy.alberta.ca (accessed on May 6, 2011). See also Don Whiteley, "Oil Exports to Asia Drive Expansion Plans at B.C. Ports in Vancouver and Kitimat," *Vancouver Sun*, December 1, 2009.

Summary and Conclusion

Climate legislation in Canada has thus far been led by the provinces. Though provincial initiatives are an important step toward finally reducing carbon emissions in Canada, the Canadian federal government will face the challenge of coordinating these efforts in implementing national legislation. In addition, conflicting regional interests will present Canada with a dilemma going forward. With natural resource production–based economies that provide fewer avenues for painless transition to sustainable development, provinces such as Alberta face a high GDP cost of greenhouse gas mitigation in the medium term. Existing high levels of renewable generation in many provinces provide fewer opportunities for GHG reductions from the electricity sector. However, Canada will face intense pressure to act immediately to reduce the probability of catastrophic climate change. As we detail in chapter 5, integration of Canada's GHG regulations with those of the United States could reduce the cost of compliance with an international regime and smooth out some of the regional distributional effects of a cap-and-trade system highlighted in this chapter.

4

Mexico

Mexico was the world's 11th largest emitter of greenhouse gases (GHGs) in 2005, accounting for 1.7 percent of the world total. While Mexico's global share is small, its total emissions are growing rapidly. Between 1990 and 2005, GHG emissions in Mexico increased by 40 percent, more than in the other two North American Free Trade Agreement (NAFTA) countries, despite a modest improvement in emissions intensity.[1] In 2005, Mexico's three largest sources of emissions were transport, which contributed 131 million metric tons (mmt) of CO_2 equivalent (CO_2e); power, which contributed 121 mmt of CO_2e; and oil and gas, which contributed 95 mmt of CO_2e. Together, these three sectors constituted about 60 percent of Mexico's total emissions (see figure 4.1).

At the 14th session of the UN Framework Convention on Climate Change (UNFCCC) Conference of Parties (COP-14) in Poznan, Poland, in December 2008, Mexico announced its intention to reduce emissions 50 percent from 2002 levels by 2050, contingent upon developed-country assistance. At the 15th session, in Copenhagen, Mexico announced its commitment to reducing emissions 51 mmt below business-as-usual levels by 2012 (equivalent to about a 6.4 percent cut) and 30 percent below business as usual by 2020 (equivalent to about 250 mmt of CO_2e) (UNFCCC 2010a).[2]

Given the source of Mexico's GHG emissions, significant changes will be required in energy production, distribution, and consumption for Mexico to

---

1. World Resources Institute, Climate Access Indicators Tool, http://cait.wri.org (accessed on June 8, 2011).

2. The 2012 percentage emissions reduction estimate and the 2020 absolute emissions reduction estimate are calculated by the authors based on business-as-usual emissions projections in Centro Mario Molina (2008).

Figure 4.1 Greenhouse gas emissions in Mexico, by sector, 2005

million metric tons

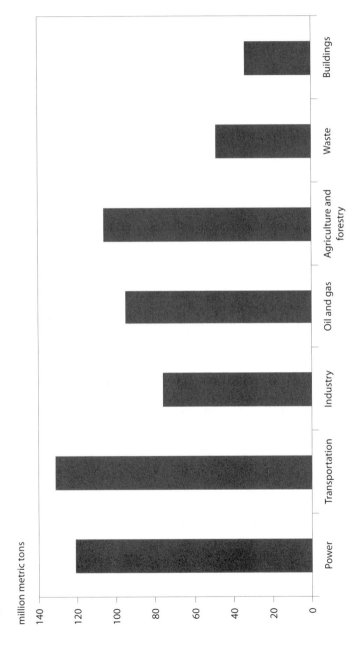

Source: Centro Mario Molina (2008).

meet its own ambitious climate policy goals. Under a business-as-usual scenario, power emissions are expected to double by 2030, driven by the expansion of fossil fuel–based generation, particularly from natural gas.[3] Transport emissions are expected to grow by 70 percent, as automobile ownership expands. The prospective growth in Mexican GHG emissions underscores the importance of reducing Mexico's wasteful gasoline and other energy subsidies, which currently reduce incentives for energy efficiency and renewable energy production, at both firm and individual levels.

Despite its ambitious plans to sharply cut GHG emissions, Mexico will have difficulty meeting its targets without new sources of financing. Mexico is already the fourth-largest recipient of Clean Development Mechanism (CDM) funding, which delivers about 9 mmt in reductions every year.[4] These reductions, however, are small in comparison to Mexico's short-term goal of reducing emissions by 51 mmt and its medium-term goal of reducing emissions 30 percent below business-as-usual levels by 2020. In addition, the CDM is not well designed to fund projects in the transportation sector, where monitoring nonstationary pollution sources and determining additionality—whether the emissions reductions from the project exceed those that would have occurred without the project—is cumbersome (Gruetter 2007, 2011). Currently, there are only two transport-related CDM projects out of a total of 124 CDM projects in Mexico. Nor is CDM funding especially useful in forestry activities: over 80 percent of emissions reduction potential in forestry lies in activities that fall outside the scope of the CDM, such as forest management, where the impact on GHG emissions is hard to quantify (Tudela 2003).

In addition, Mexico's climate initiatives have been constrained by its energy policies. Few leaders have dared challenge constitutional provisions that grant PEMEX, Mexico's state-owned oil company, a monopoly on the exploitation and development of energy resources and bar foreign firms from ownership of oil and gas reserves. Energy reform is one of the most sensitive and intractable issues in Mexican politics, and it has been for generations. Although recent reforms allow incentive-based service contracts with the private sector, opinion polls continue to show strong majorities disapproving of foreign investment in Mexico's natural resources.

What does this situation mean for climate change policy? Because government officials have long regarded PEMEX as a cash cow of the federal government, they have drained funds that PEMEX could have invested in new production and distribution networks of both petroleum and renewable resources. Milking PEMEX also has enabled Mexican politicians to postpone fiscal reforms to broaden the tax base, which is an even more urgent task for Mexico than energy reform. As a result, Mexico produces less energy than it

---

3. Oil and gas emissions growth will be driven primarily by fugitive methane emissions. See Centro Mario Molina (2008).

4. UNFCCC, Expected Average Annual CERs from Registered Projects by Host Party, http://cdm.unfccc.int (accessed on February 1, 2011).

could or should, relies too much on carbon-intensive resources for power generation, and produces too little energy from cleaner, renewable resources. We discuss these problems in more detail toward the end of this chapter.

Multilateral negotiations have recently made progress toward international financing of climate programs, but uncertainties remain. At the COP-15 in Copenhagen, the rich industrial countries promised $100 billion to help fund GHG mitigation policies in developing countries, and the Cancún Agreements at the COP-16 in 2010 established the Green Climate Fund to disburse a portion of this money. However, it is yet unclear how much of this money will materialize—particularly with the US Congress reluctant to earmark funds for climate assistance in the near future.

Mexico must also navigate between the current pressures arising from inaction by the United States and Canada and the potential future pressures that could arise from action on climate change. Currently, the legislative stalemate in the United States and Canada has reduced the incentives—both political and financial—for Mexico to follow through on its ambitious emissions reduction targets. Once the United States and Canada adopt national climate programs, however, an international reserve allowance program or similar measure is likely to be included in the legislation, particularly in the United States. Even with limited emissions allowance trading, there would be a number of options for linking Mexico to the climate regimes of its northern neighbors, including carbon offset trading, if Mexico invested in the requisite infrastructure for measurement, reporting, and verification. Mexico would have a strong incentive to do so to establish channels for financing its climate change mitigation efforts.

Accomplishments to Date

In the past five years, Mexico has undertaken a number of planning initiatives aimed at the eventual achievement of its climate change goals. Unlike the action taken by its northern neighbors, most action to date on climate change in Mexico has been concentrated at the federal level. Until recently, the Mexican federal government exclusively set environmental policy, and it still has much more power to do so than the United States or Canada. With the assistance of the federal government, however, local and regional climate action is beginning to take root in Mexico as well. Veracruz, Mexico City, and Nuevo León have already completed climate plans in consultation with the Mexican government, and Mexico City has undertaken significant mass transit projects that have addressed greenhouse gas emissions from transportation (discussed below).[5]

In 2007, the Mexican government published its *National Strategy on Climate*

5. Government of Nuevo León, Programa de Acción ante el Cambio Climático, www.nl.gob.mx (accessed on May 7, 2011) and Government of Veracruz, Programa Veracruzano ante el Cambio Climático, 2009, Xalapa.

Change, which estimated the mitigation potential of a number of broad actions, including the installation of combined heat and power facilities, energy-efficiency improvements for PEMEX, installation of renewable electricity capacity, and sustainable forest management (ICCC 2007). The 2007 document formed the basis of Mexico's 2009 Special Climate Change Program (PECC) (ICCC 2009).

Introduced in the lead-up to the December 2009 Copenhagen conference, the PECC sets short- and long-term mitigation goals, pledging to reduce emissions approximately 6.4 percent (51 mmt) below business-as-usual levels in 2012 and 50 percent below 2002 levels in 2050.[6] The PECC also lays out a number of actions that would contribute toward meeting the 2012 target and identifies the agencies responsible for their implementation, the Secretariat of Environment and Natural Resources (Semarnat) and the National Energy Secretariat (SENER). Proposed actions include management of landfill gas; expansion of sustainable forest management, including expansion of payment for environmental services; self-supply schemes for renewable energy; and wind power generation by the Federal Electricity Commission (CFE), Mexico's national electricity utility.

Mexico has also taken a number of actions that shore up capacity for climate change mitigation. The most recent was in 2011, when Mexico's General Law of Ecological Balance and Environmental Protection was amended to define climate change and give environmental agencies the authority to implement mitigation strategies.[7] In November 2008, the Law for the Use of Renewable Energy and Financing the Energy Transition (Laerfte) came into force, establishing a $250 million per year fund for renewables, a $37 million per year fund for emerging technologies, an 8 percent target by 2012 for renewable energy generation (excluding large hydroelectric facilities), standard contracts for the purchase of renewable power by CFE, and rules for the purchase of surplus energy from renewable self-supply and cogeneration projects. Another important initiative passed at the same time is the Law for the Sustainable Use of Energy (LASE). The National Plan for the Sustainable Use of Energy created under LASE enumerates measures to reduce energy use from transport and appliances, including new fuel economy standards, new appliance standards, and the promotion of efficient lighting (SENER 2009).

In addition to these institutional reforms, Mexico has taken concrete steps to establish renewable generation facilities. Mexico's current energy plan, the Energy Sector Program 2007–12, lays out a goal of 26 percent of electricity from renewable energy generation by 2012 (including all hydroelectric facilities), and the 2010 National Energy Strategy sets a goal of 35 percent of elec-

---

6. An approximate business-as-usual projection for Mexican emissions was obtained by multiplying Mexican GHG emissions during the last year for which data were available, 2006, by the annual emissions growth projected by the US Energy Information Administration (EIA 2010).

7. Mexico Congress, Decreto por el que se adiciona una fracción XVII al Artículo 3⁰. de la Ley General del Equilibrio Ecológico y la Protección al Ambiente, January 28, 2011, www.bdlaw.com (accessed on May 8, 2011). See also Torres Landa and Yanez Vega (2011).

tricity from "clean" sources by 2024. CFE plans to meet this goal through new nuclear and wind generation.[8] The National Energy Strategy also promises a 1 percent decrease in the annual rate of electricity consumption growth.

Mexico has established two "La Venta" wind farms and is constructing a third. Though the first was fairly small, the second has a capacity of 83 megawatts (MW), and the third is expected to have a capacity of 103 MW.[9] According to a proposed federal plan, the Mexican government intends to install 7 gigawatts (GW) of additional wind and geothermal energy by 2014, which amounts to one-eighth of current generating capacity, enough to fulfill Mexico's 2012 renewable electricity target if combined with existing hydroelectric capacity.[10]

Since the mid-1990s, the Mexican government also has made modest progress on deforestation. Between 1995 and 2000, 960,000 hectares were reforested, sequestering 71 mmt of carbon. Subsidies that encouraged clearing of land for agriculture were eliminated (Tudela 2003). Under new regulations, land use changes require an environmental impact assessment, a sustainable forestry management plan, and even stricter requirements for forests within Natural Protected Areas. While the Mexican Forest Fund, established in 2003, has faced some setbacks, payment to prevent logging and land clearing has proven effective so far. Between 2003 and 2005, less than 0.01 percent of the land paid for by the fund was deforested. The deforestation rate in the rest of the country was 1 percent per year (Karousakis 2007).

In addition, the Mexican legislature has been active on climate change. In March 2010, Senator Alberto Cárdenas Jiménez introduced a bill that would authorize market-based mechanisms for climate change mitigation, including a cap-and-trade system and a carbon tax. Although the legislation has not yet passed, it represents a step forward. The bill is described in appendix 4A.

A number of partnerships with outside institutions facilitate Mexico's climate change efforts. Between 2008 and 2009, the World Bank approved a total of $2.7 billion in loans to support environmental sustainability and climate change mitigation in Mexico.[11] Of that total, $1.5 billion will support the PECC by contributing toward institutions, regulations, and monitoring capacity to reduce GHG emissions from urban transport and to promote clean and renewable energy. As part of this initiative, the World Bank will help finance the Federal Support Program for Mass Transit (PROTRAM), which combines

---

8. Robert Campbell, "Mexico Eyes up to 10 New Nuclear Plants by 2028," Reuters, May 12, 2010.

9. "Iberdrola Renovables to Build La Venta III Wind Farm in Mexico," *Energy Business Review*, March 11, 2009.

10. The Energy Information Administration reports that Mexico had 56 GW of installed capacity in 2007. See Energy Information Administration, Country Analysis Brief: Mexico, www.eia.gov/cabs/Mexico/Full.html (accessed on June 8, 2011).

11. "The World Bank Supports Mexico's Efforts to Combat Climate Change," *NAFTA Works*, November 2009, 2.

bus and train transit projects with measures such as congestion pricing to reduce the proliferation of cars. The World Bank loans will also support renewable energy and energy-efficiency measures.[12] Another $700 billion in loans authorized in November 2010 will support renewable energy, sustainable forestry management, sustainable housing, and increased use of efficient home appliances.[13]

In conjunction with the Environmental Defense Fund, PEMEX operated an experimental emissions trading system for SO_2 and GHGs between 2001 and 2002, reducing CO_2e emissions by 3 mmt, or 1 percent below 1999 levels (EIA 2003).[14] Crude oil production increased by 1.6 percent during this time.[15] The trading system had 25 participants, including refineries, production facilities, gas processing facilities, and petrochemical complexes. The success of this trading system appeared to lay the groundwork for further efforts to reduce emissions, but surprisingly there has been little follow-up. At the end of the pilot project, PEMEX discussed pursuit of a 10 percent GHG reduction over 1999 levels by 2009, but never achieved this goal, as the pilot project was dropped. Similarly, Semarnat and SENER discussed an integrated emissions trading system involving PEMEX and CFE in 2002, but these discussions never moved past the preliminary phase.

The United States Agency for International Development (USAID) supported the mapping of the Oaxacan wind corridor, allowing private firms, including US firms, to site wind projects in the Ventosa area, one of the best wind generation sites in the world. USAID has since gone on to fund mapping projects in Baja California, Chihuahua, Sonora, and Yucatán. The mapping of northern Baja California has been particularly instrumental in encouraging wind development in the high-potential La Rumorosa region (Wood 2010). In addition, USAID (2009) published a comparative analysis in 2009 of regulatory frameworks for wind energy in both countries.

The Inter-American Development Bank supports the Sustainable Energy and Climate Change Initiative (SECCI), which offers project-specific technical assistance and investment grants in the areas of renewable energy, bioenergy, energy efficiency, access to carbon markets, and adaptation. The SECCI's policy-based loans support national programs for climate change mitigation and adaptation. Mexico received its first loan, worth $2 million, in December 2008, to fund the formulation and implementation of its national climate

---

12. World Bank, Program Document for a Proposed Framework for Green Growth Development Policy Loan in the Amount of US$1.504 Billion to the United Mexican States, September 16, 2009, www.worldbank.org (accessed May 23, 2011).

13. Dow Jones/Factiva, "Mexico to Receive $700 Billion in World Bank Loans for Climate Change," November 23, 2010.

14. See also PEMEX, PEMEX's Internal Market for Emissions Trading, slide presentation, September 3, 2008, www.ccap.org (accessed on May 7, 2011).

15. PEMEX, *Statistical Yearbook 2003*, www.ri.pemex.com (accessed on May 31, 2011).

change strategy. In addition, the SECCI supports Mexico City's Bordo Poniente landfill gas capture and electricity generation project (Wood 2010).

Mexico also has worked with the Global Environmental Facility (GEF) to promote renewable energy. The Large-Scale Renewable Energy Development Project funded by the GEF provides $20 million in performance-based financial incentives to the La Venta III installation.[16] This initiative allows CFE to pay only for the avoided cost of conventional generation—making the La Venta III wind farm cost-competitive with fossil fuel–based generation—while the GEF makes up the difference. In addition, the GEF granted $50 million for a hybrid solar and natural gas plant in Sonora and $5 million for technical assistance to incorporate renewable energy (CEC 2007).

Near-Term Challenges

Mexico faces a steep business-as-usual emissions growth trajectory. If no further action is taken in Mexico, emissions are projected to increase 62 percent by 2030, with the biggest emitters being power, transport, and industry. Power emissions are expected to double from 121 million metric tons in 2005 to 240 mmt CO_2e in 2030, and transport emissions are predicted to grow 2.2 percent annually, from 131 mmt in 2005 to 225 mmt in 2030 (Centro Mario Molina 2008). As a result, Mexico will need to improve energy efficiency relative to the baseline scenario while developing less GHG-intensive sources of energy.

Like the United States, Mexico has a fossil fuel–based economy. In 2006, 92 percent of energy consumption came from fossil fuels—55 percent from petroleum, 32 percent from natural gas, and 5 percent from coal (EIA 2009). Most electricity generation also comes from fossil fuels, with 9 percent of generation from coal, 36 percent from natural gas, and 29 percent from fuel oil. The share of natural gas in electricity generation has increased rapidly, growing at an average of 16 percent per year between 1997 and 2007.[17] Less than one-quarter of Mexican electricity comes from renewables (21 percent from hydroelectric), and 3 percent comes from nuclear power (SENER 2007).

The Centro Mario Molina (2008) estimates that Mexico has the potential to reduce emissions 25 percent from 2005 levels by 2030 using existing and near-commercial technologies. These reductions include an increase in renewable share to 50 percent of generation by 2030, a shift in electricity generation from oil to natural gas, and installation of a smart grid system.[18] In order to

---

16. Laerfte's fund is separate from the GEF initiative, which was implemented two years before the Laerfte passed the legislature, although they both follow the same model (Mata 2006).

17. This growth largely arises from natural gas cogeneration, which has replaced fuel oil–fired plants.

18. The researchers estimate a modest increase in solar, geothermal, and hydroelectric power relative to Mexico's potential. However, they assume that Mexico makes better use of "stranded" wind generation sites in order to exceed its current calculated wind potential (Centro Mario Molina 2008).

reduce transport emissions, Mexico will also need to embrace new standards for fuel efficiency, develop sustainable biofuels, and expand public transport. These investments can be made most cheaply in the near future. Much of Mexico's capital stock has not yet been built, so the sooner investments are made, the lower the cost of replacing existing infrastructure.

PEMEX has a great deal of potential for emissions reductions. The introduction of cogeneration at PEMEX facilities could provide over 6 percent of Mexico's current installed power capacity (Centro Mario Molina 2008). This contribution would help Mexico adjust to declining oil production due to the rapid depletion of some of its major oil fields. Mexico will need to increasingly rely on natural gas for its energy needs and will need to refocus its energy infrastructure accordingly (Selin and VanDeveer 2009). To that end, gas that is currently flared and vented could be captured and consumed, offsetting natural gas imports while eliminating a significant source of GHG emissions (Johnson et al. 2010).

Nevertheless, Mexico faces a number of challenges. These include budgetary problems at all levels of government; a rigid government monopoly on electricity; the proliferation of old, inefficient vehicles; and the difficulty of halting deforestation. Below, we explain these challenges in more detail.

Financing for the Federal Government

Despite the international financing that Mexico has received to date, its goals are too great in scope to achieve without additional domestic and international channels of support. The Centro Mario Molina, in a report published in collaboration with McKinsey and Company, and estimates that to achieve a 54 percent reduction from business-as-usual levels by 2030—a goal roughly consistent with Mexico's Copenhagen targets—Mexico will need to invest about $7.2 billion a year in 2011–15, and about $18 billion a year in 2026–30. These amounts, which correspond to approximately a 3 percent increase in Mexico's economy-wide capital investment, swamp the amount of international financing received by Mexico to date for climate change programs (Centro Mario Molina 2008).

Internally, Mexico faces a number of fiscal impediments going forward. One of its major sources of revenue, PEMEX, faces major challenges in financing new exploration and development. Meanwhile, substantial energy subsidies cut into the funds necessary for investments in and upgrades to Mexico's energy infrastructure. It is also difficult for local governments to obtain funding. We discuss these obstacles below.

The PEMEX Challenge

Part of the funding problem for energy investments can be attributed to Mexico's oil laws and regulations affecting energy resources. Articles 27 and 28 of the 1917 Mexican Constitution prohibit foreign investment in strategic energy sectors. Foreign firms can contract their services to PEMEX, but they cannot own any of the oil produced, which substantially discourages foreign participation in the oil and gas sector (Hufbauer and Schott 2005).

Although recent reforms allow incentive-based service contracts with the private sector, constitutional constraints bar foreign firms from ownership of reserves or hydrocarbons produced.[19] Tax policies that siphon off oil earnings from PEMEX, the state monopoly, to the federal treasury reduce funds available for investment in energy production and distribution. Among other problems, these factors result in inefficient and limited production of oil and natural gas, heavy reliance on carbon-intensive fuel oil for power generation, and limited flows of natural gas and electricity between the United States and Mexico.

Attempting to address this problem, Mexico's 2007–12 Energy Sector Program includes goals to expand competition in nonstrategic areas and promote "changes to the legal framework" in order to promote technological investment in hydrocarbons (SENER 2007). In addition, the Mexican Petroleum Law enacted in November 2008 aims to provide new incentives for foreign investment. The law grants new authority to PEMEX's board of directors, allowing it to hire private contractors more simply and quickly. The board of directors may also pay variable compensation to private contractors, increasing pay if work is completed ahead of schedule or new technology is transferred to PEMEX (Serra 2009).

Despite these modest energy reforms, however, constitutional barriers continue to discourage efforts to promote foreign investment in offshore exploration. Sidney Weintraub (2010) points out that large oil producers are not interested in a bonus; rather, they prefer risk contracts in which they bear the cost of exploration but reap the reward if the venture is successful. Under the current framework, companies cannot obtain these contracts—and the political climate is unlikely to allow this to change in the near future. Mexican service contracts also do not allow private oil companies to record reserves with the US Securities and Exchange Commission, further reducing incentives for exploration—companies can obtain credit against recorded reserves (Weintraub 2010).

These constraints inhibit access to foreign technology and finance needed to exploit deep-water oil fields. In theory, the threat of diminished oil revenues could strengthen the government's interest in reducing fossil fuel subsidies and promoting alternative sources of energy. However, lack of revenues will also cause further shortfalls of money for the energy investments necessary to transition to lower-carbon energy sources. Investment in national energy utilities already imposes a significant strain on the federal budget.

With PEMEX as the cash cow of the federal government, there is a trade-off between expenditures for national programs and infrastructure investments in energy exploration, development, and distribution. The federal govern-

---

19. Amy Guthrie, "Mexico Supreme Court Allows New Private Service Oil Contracts," *Wall Street Journal*, December 8, 2010.

ment is dependent on oil earnings for a substantial share (over one-third) of its budget.[20] The ratio of nonoil tax revenues to GDP is among the lowest among Organization for Economic Cooperation and Development countries. However, the diversion of funds to Mexico City has led to underinvestment in energy production and distribution. Engaging foreign oil firms in Mexican projects, though it requires legal finesse, is thus crucial for Mexico's energy future. Without major new investments, especially in offshore fields, Mexico could become a net importer of oil in a few years (EIA 2010). The United States derives 10 percent of its oil imports from Mexico and would be affected as well if Mexican production is diverted from exports to domestic consumption.[21]

Falling oil revenues took an observable toll on Mexico's ability to obtain credit in 2009, prompting Fitch Ratings to lower Mexico's and PEMEX's credit ratings to BBB, just one step above the lowest investment category.[22] At the end of 2009, PEMEX had $50 billion in debt, more than any other oil company.[23] Production has since risen, and offshore output has stabilized, alleviating short-term worries as of mid-2011.[24] Yet long-term fiscal health remains a concern. In February 2011, Standard and Poor expressed concern over PEMEX's "unfavorable reserve replacement rate."[25] If oil revenues fall again, Mexico and PEMEX may find it increasingly costly to obtain lending for new investments in the infrastructure necessary to improve efficiency and reduce carbon emissions from energy production.

Fossil Fuel Subsidies

Another funding challenge for Mexico is that enormous energy subsidies have further drained government coffers. Although politically challenging, removal of electricity and fossil fuel subsidies could reduce the drain on Mexican public revenues, while at the same time creating incentives to conserve energy. Residential and agricultural consumers pay only a fraction of actual costs, reducing incentives for energy efficiency. Most subsidies (over 90 percent) go to consumers above the poverty line, and about 40 percent of subsidies go to the top three income deciles, benefitting consumers who would otherwise be

20. The figure is from the Thomson Reuters Datastream Database, 2010.

21. Energy Information Administration, US Imports by Country of Origin, http://tonto.eia.doe.gov (accessed on November 1, 2010).

22. Andres Martinez, "Mexico: PEMEX May Sell Net $3 Billion of Debt in 2010," Bloomberg, December 3, 2009.

23. "Update: Mexico PEMEX Cuts 4Q Net Loss to MXN16.6B on Exports," *Wall Street Journal*, March 1, 2010.

24. Robert Campbell, "Mexico Oil Output Hits 8-Month High in January," Reuters, February 24, 2011.

25. "S&P Highlights Pemex 'Unfavorable' Reserve Replacement Rate," Business News Americas, February 14, 2011, http://member.bnamericas.com (accessed on March 12, 2011).

able to pay the full cost of electricity (Komives et al. 2009). Large industrial, commercial, and municipal electricity consumers are charged higher rates and thus partly subsidize residential and agricultural electricity consumption under the federal electricity system, but even these higher rates are not quite high enough to recover costs (Garten Rothkopf 2009). Meanwhile, industrial and commercial electricity users are increasingly contracting for renewable power from private companies under self-supply arrangements.[26]

Electricity tariffs are determined by an interagency group including CFE, SENER, the Ministry of Finance, and the Energy Regulatory Commission (CRE), and they are set below the level required for CFE to recoup costs (ESMAP 2004). To offset the cost to CFE, the federal government credits the subsidies against the required payment—the *aprovechamientos*—of 8 percent of CFE's assets. When the required subsidies exceed the *aprovechamientos*, as they have since 2000, CFE instead uses its own capital to pay the subsidies. This practice has cut into funds available for investment in new and replacement equipment, which has hurt productivity and contributed to rising operations and maintenance costs (Garten Rothkopf 2009).

The total cost to the government of petroleum and electricity subsidies was about $20 billion in 2008, or almost 2 percent of GDP (Weintraub 2010). Removal of these subsidies would free up substantial sums that could be invested instead into new, more efficient facilities. In addition, the subsequent increase in the price of energy would create incentives to conserve. The total carbon impact of removing fossil fuel subsidies is estimated to be 50 mt CO_2e in 2020, or about 6 percent of total emissions under a business-as-usual-scenario (Centro Mario Molina 2008).

Fossil fuel subsidies are heavily ingrained in government policy, however, and will be very difficult to remove. Although Mexico's energy minister indicated in 2008 that gasoline and diesel prices would be gradually raised to US levels,[27] such fiscal rectitude soon dissipated amid fears that fuel price increases would put pressure on Mexico's inflation rate (Weintraub 2010). Moreover, removal of subsidies would require a comprehensive program to increase the credit and technical capacity for small and medium-size enterprises, which tend to have relatively high energy intensities and to use older equipment, to allow them to adapt to higher energy prices. These firms generally have a difficult time obtaining access to technical knowledge and financing for upgrades.

Financing for Local Governments

Local governments also lack funding for environmental programs and enforcement. Municipalities depend for income on property taxes, which tend to be low and poorly collected; the value-added tax paid on goods and services,

---

26. In order to contract for independently produced power, the firms must own shares in the independent power producers.

27. Lynn Brezosky, "U.S. Gas Now a Big Bargain in Mexico," *San Antonio Express-News*, June 17, 2008.

which generates more income, is collected and administered by the central government. The Mexican government prohibits municipalities from raising capital outside the domestic market, so localities tend to depend on revenue sharing from federal and state governments. This revenue is uncertain, as it is determined by legislative decree on a year-by-year basis. Only 3 percent of the taxes collected by the Mexican federal government are returned to municipalities. Communities have the option of borrowing from Mexico's National Bank of Public Works and Services for environmental infrastructure project loans, but most cannot reliably repay the principal and interest due to their limited and inconsistent revenue flows (Hufbauer and Schott 2005).

Role of Government Electricity Monopolies

Under the Mexican Constitution, the electricity sector has been federally owned since the 1960s. While private producers have some space to obtain self-supply contracts (between a generator and an entity that owns shares in the generator) in addition to contracts with CFE, their role remains limited. In theory, the government's administrative power over the electricity market could make it easier for the government to force electricity producers to meet government goals regarding the climate change impact of electricity production. In practice, however, the state-owned energy firms have been slow to comply with environmental mandates in the absence of effective sanctions.

The government electricity monopoly is subject to a number of conditions that inhibit the development of renewable electricity resources. First, CFE is required to purchase power at the lowest possible cost (Garrison 2010, Johnson et al. 2010). Renewable power is often unable to compete with the more efficient fossil fuel–based generation due to high start-up costs. The 2008 reforms require CFE to incorporate environmental externalities into the cost of electricity, in order to make renewable power more cost-competitive relative to fossil fuels, but it remains to be seen whether the reforms will actually spur CFE to purchase more renewable electricity. Second, government electricity contracts are long term, often thirty years or more, and involve complex negotiations with both generators and labor unions. This lack of flexibility discourages purchases of electricity produced using emerging technologies as well as contracts with smaller producers (Huacuz 2007). As a result of these constraints, new capacity commissioned by CFE has centered overwhelmingly on natural gas combined cycle plants (Garten Rothkopf 2009).

Self-supply producers—generators that produce electricity for their own consumption or for consumption by their shareholders—are ideally suited to developing nascent renewable technologies, as they are free from price constraints imposed by CFE. Indeed, these producers have driven the growth of renewable electricity to date (Wood 2010). However, the law prevents this electricity from being sold except to companies that own a share in the generator. Self-supply producers located far from the consumers—such as those in the wind-rich region of Oaxaca—are forced to use CFE's transmission network, for which CFE charges a fee that can amount to 15 to 30 percent of final electricity prices (Lokey 2008). Partly as a consequence of these factors, only 1 GW out of 51 GW of total Mexican electricity capacity is generated by self-supply or small projects (Garten Rothkopf 2009). Liberalization or privatization of the electricity industry is unlikely in the near term given the hard political and constitutional constraints (Hufbauer and Schott 2005). In order for the industry to expand further, however, barriers to contracting with renewable electricity producers will need to be overcome.

Emissions from Transportation

Mexico has one of the most carbon-intensive transport sectors in the region, partly because the country has the highest motorization rate in Latin America: 107 vehicles per 1,000 inhabitants (World Bank 2009). Government policies contribute to this trend. Fuel subsidies keep prices low, reducing incentives to use other means of transport. Policies to curb automobile use such as Mexico City's Hoy No Circula program, which restricts drivers with certain license plate numbers from driving on certain days, have actually exacerbated the growth of automobile ownership, as some people have purchased additional cars in order to circumvent the ban (Davis 2008).

The environmental problems posed by the growing number of cars are worsened by an increasing share of older vehicles, for which there is inadequate environmental regulation. Part of this problem lies in the public transportation system. Mexico's bus fleet is aging, in part due to a system in which individual owners of buses contract with the federal government rather than the government purchasing and owning the buses themselves (World Bank 2009). This system also leads to a greater number of buses than necessary. However, the public transport situation is rapidly improving—at least in the Federal District.[28] One-third of daily public transportation rides in Mexico City are taken on electric transport, Metrobus, or city buses, and additional investment in clean public transport, including a new Metrobus line, is in the pipeline. Metrobus burns low-sulfur diesel fuel and is estimated by the Mexico City government to have cut carbon emissions by 80,000 metric tons per year. A financing arrangement that makes the contractor responsible for construction and maintenance costs for 10 years allows the city to afford the new Metrobus project. However, the overwhelming majority of public transport use still involves aging, emissions-intensive minibuses.[29]

Many older vehicles are also private vehicles imported from the United States, where they would otherwise be scrapped. Under NAFTA requirements, Mexico had to begin phasing out its prior ban on used car imports starting

---

28. Mexico City accounts for about 20 percent of nationwide transport emissions and 9 percent of overall nationwide emissions. See Mexico City (2008).

29. Mary Cuddehe, "Improvements to Mobility in Choked Capital," *Financial Times*, March 31, 2010, 4.

in 2009; restrictions must be completely removed by 2019. In August 2005, President Vicente Fox got a head start on this requirement when he signed a decree allowing 10- to 15-year-old used vehicles to enter Mexico. Between November 2005 and December 2008, 3 million 10- to 15-year-old vehicles were imported from the United States, increasing Mexico's vehicle stock by 10 percent. In March 2008, Mexico banned imports of cars over 10 years old, but a substantial used car market still remains—and under NAFTA's requirements, the ban is only temporary. Lucas Davis and Matthew Kahn (2008) found that current policies increased the total number of cars in circulation, as cars that would have otherwise been scrapped were kept on the road.[30]

Problem of Deforestation

Deforestation contributes about 14 percent of Mexico's greenhouse gas emissions (Johnson et al. 2010), and Mexico's 2007 climate change plan specified more abatement potential in forestation than in any other sector. New land use regulations and significant replantings have decreased the deforestation rate from 340,000 hectares of forest per year, the average annual rate between 1990 and 2000, to 260,000 hectares of forest per year between 2000 and 2005.[31] However, this still gives Mexico one of the highest deforestation rates in the Western Hemisphere. Forest cover in Mexico has been steadily decreasing since 1995 (see figure 4.2), and it is estimated that 30 percent of the timber from forests is illegally logged (World Bank 2010).

Reduced emissions from deforestation and forest degradation (REDD) are difficult to achieve due to lack of incentives for farmers, who are poor, vulnerable, and risk averse. Forest preservation is not sufficiently profitable compared with agriculture and use of land as pasture, and price signals are not sufficient to induce farmers to switch professions, as alternative jobs are not available in the regions where small-scale farmers have established homes (Hufbauer and Schott 2005). Mexico also lacks sufficient monitoring and enforcement capacity to address deforestation, and the boundaries of national parks and reserves are poorly enforced (Johnson et al. 2010, Alix-Garcia et al. 2005). Because failure to enforce the law makes land less scarce than it should be, market signals to farmers to intensify production are lost (Alix-Garcia et al. 2005).

---

30. Davis and Kahn (2008) also found that a higher gasoline tax in the United States would present a substantial likelihood of leakage to Mexico, as it would lower the price of used cars exported to Mexico. On the other hand, higher Corporate Average Fuel Economy (CAFE) standards would cause US demand for used cars to increase, increasing the price of used cars exported to Mexico and reducing the size of the Mexican used car market.

31. United Nations Food and Agriculture Organization, ResourceSTAT, http://faostat.fao.org/ (accessed on May 6, 2011).

Figure 4.2   Forest area in Mexico, 1995–2008

thousands of hectares

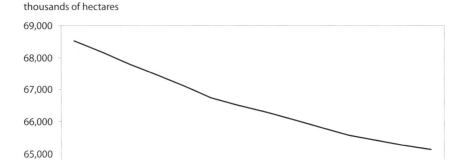

Source: United Nations Food and Agriculture Organization, ResourceSTAT, http://faostat.fao.org (accessed on May 6, 2011).

Can NAFTA Help Achieve Mexico's Carbon Reduction Goals?

Although Mexico has proven more willing than many other developing countries to take on climate change commitments, it is unlikely that its ambitious climate change goals will be achieved without technical and financial assistance from developed countries. Sources of funding are as yet uncertain, and the UN climate regime is likely to focus assistance on the poorest countries rather than middle-income countries like Mexico. As a consequence, Mexico will need to look to its neighbors and NAFTA partners, the United States and Canada, to play a role in funding its transition to a low-carbon economy and in overcoming the barriers inherent to its political and economic system. The cost to Mexico of reducing GHG emissions is likely to far outstrip politically feasible financial transfers from these countries, however. Moreover, the United States and Canada might be reluctant to subsidize the carbon reductions of a country that heavily subsidizes fossil fuels.

Instead, the United States and Canada should look to support Mexico both directly and indirectly through existing policies and programs. The challenge is to develop mutually reinforcing policies that help each NAFTA partner achieve its climate change goals in a period of tight budget constraints.

Given the integration of North American energy markets, an integrated NAFTA-wide approach would be preferable. Though near-term prospects for a North American carbon trading system are not bright, the eventual establishment of such a regime could provide some funds through the sale of carbon reductions. Under the American Clean Energy and Security Act, there was a possibility of selling carbon offsets if Mexico could establish a sectoral baseline. Such a system would prove less onerous to Mexico than an economy-wide cap-and-trade program, and the sale of offsets could potentially raise needed revenue. Although the offsets would not provide reductions in addition to those realized by developed-country cap-and-trade programs—one would not wish to double-count offset reductions toward both the United States and Mexican emissions reduction programs, for example—they could provide funding to start Mexico on a path to a lower-carbon economy. The Mexican government could work with the private sector in order to establish a carbon accounting system to sell offsets abroad. Centro Mario Molina (2008) estimates that Mexican offsets could be worth $2 billion per year by 2030, assuming a $50 per ton carbon price.

In the near term, a less ambitious approach may be feasible. Positive steps can be taken using existing legislation and existing institutions. Two specific areas merit priority attention: production of renewable energy and REDD initiatives. Mexico needs broad-based reform of the energy sector; in the meantime, the United States could provide a market for Mexican renewable electricity generators. Indeed, several renewable electricity projects have developed along the US-Mexico border. Growing demand for renewable electricity in California and other US border states as a result of state renewable portfolio standards provides Mexican border states with an attractive market for solar and wind electricity generated in Mexico.

Before Mexico can export at scale, transmission capacity must be improved. Whereas Canada has over 100 export transmission lines to the United States, Mexico has only 9 (Pugua 2007). Duncan Wood (2010) argues that lack of transmission capacity is the single largest obstacle that Mexico faces in taking advantage of this market. Additional cross-border transmission would allow firms conducting renewables projects to take advantage of economies of scale; several firms have already located generation sites along both sides of the border in the hopes of scaling up generation for both markets. Such economies of scale would lower the cost of compliance with state renewable standards, make solar and wind power more competitive relative to conventional fuels, and accelerate the development of renewable infrastructure on both sides of the border.

Sale of renewable electricity and renewable electricity certificates (RECs) to US states that have renewable portfolio standards could be a means of getting around CFE's requirement to purchase power at least cost.[32] These market mechanisms could lead CFE to generate more renewable electricity, if increased revenue from renewable electricity or RECs compensates for the extra cost of renewable electricity relative to fossil fuel–powered generation. In order for RECs to be traded internationally, compatible standards for the environmental integrity of RECs would need to be set.

---

32. See chapter 2 for a description of renewable portfolio standards in the United States.

The United States and Mexico already have taken steps toward cooperation on these issues. As part of a 2009 Bilateral Framework on Clean Energy and Climate Change, Presidents Obama and Calderón committed to address transmission and distribution obstacles between the two countries.[33] In May 2010, the two presidents launched the Cross-Border Electricity Task Force to promote a regional renewable energy market and coordinate electricity transmission and grid connections.[34] The two heads of state agreed to cooperate on smart grid standards and technology, which could help Mexico significantly increase energy efficiency. These high-level conversations should propel concrete action that over time removes barriers to renewable energy trade and development in the border region.

Conclusion

As a relatively advanced developing economy, Mexico has the potential to act on climate change and has demonstrated political will to start the process. However, it will be difficult for Mexico to make significant progress toward its long-term goals for GHG emissions without addressing its institutionalized reliance on fossil fuels for energy production and government revenue and reducing its massive and ingrained subsidies. Transportation emissions and deforestation rates also pose challenges to progress.

Contributing to many of Mexico's energy and climate change difficulties is a lack of funding for the infrastructural changes that are needed. On this front, Mexico's northern neighbors can lend assistance. NAFTA institutions, such as the Commission for Environmental Cooperation and the North American Development Bank, could be utilized to propel additional capacity building. These institutions also could study possibilities for removal of NAFTA barriers to carbon reduction in the transport sector as well as collaborate on remedial policies. We discuss specific avenues for cooperation within NAFTA in our concluding chapter.

---

33. White House, U.S.-Mexico Announce Bilateral Framework on Clean Energy and Climate Change, Office of the Press Secretary, April 16, 2009.

34. Joint statement from President Barack Obama and President Felipe Calderón, May 19, 2010, available at www.whitehouse.gov (accessed on June 8, 2011).

Appendix 4A General Climate Change Law

An ambitious bill introduced by Senator Alberto Cárdenas Jiménez (Jalisco) and supported by President Felipe Calderón attempts to transform the PECC and Mexico's Copenhagen commitments into action. The bill creates the Commission on Climate Change to establish policies and coordinate actions among different levels of government. Among other things, the commission is charged with designing a cap-and-trade system, establishing a green fund, and ensuring that federal, state, and local governments meet various goals set out in the legislation. These goals include the following:

- net zero deforestation within three years;
- in cities of over 100,000 people, zero methane emissions from waste management within five years;
- in cities of over 1 million people, mandatory vehicle inspection programs and mass transit that meets the latest emissions standards;
- a renewable electricity capacity of 40 percent of total capacity by 2030;
- no new coal generation without carbon capture and storage;
- efficient cogeneration plants for PEMEX installations; and
- zero fossil fuel subsidies by 2015.

The bill requires states and municipalities to develop climate change plans to meet these goals and threatens administrative penalties if goals are not met.

Also included are market-based mechanisms and a fund for mitigation and adaptation. Perhaps most importantly, the bill calls for an emissions registry and a carbon market. The details of both are left for the commission to establish. According to comments made by an advisor to Cárdenas, the cap-and-trade program would be established only in the context of a binding international agreement, although the text of the bill itself contains no such stipulation. The bill also promotes a carbon tax, which could vary according to the strength of other international commitments.[35]

The legislation creates a Mexican green fund for mitigation and adaptation, comprised of contributions from the federal budget; revenues from the carbon tax; contributions from foreign governments, international organizations, corporations, and individuals; sale of certified emissions reductions and emissions allowances; and administrative penalties from the act. The fund is intended to pay for PECC actions, the purchase of certified emissions reductions, adaptation in vulnerable areas, and research and development.

Although the bill holds the Mexican government accountable for reducing emissions, it places the financial burden of these reductions on the international community. The text of the bill states that Mexico's climate change

---

35. "Mexican President Calderon's Party Promotes Bill to Tax Emissions," *International Trade Reporter*, August 26, 2010.

targets presented in Copenhagen can be achieved only with "financial and technological support from developed countries at an unprecedented scale."[36] Foreign governments are expected to contribute to the green fund, though the bill does not specify the amount of funding expected.[37]

As of mid-2011, when this book was written, the law was still being discussed in the Mexican Congress. The Senate is not expected to vote on the bill until September 2011; if passed, the law will be turned over to the Chamber of Deputies.[38]

---

36. Ley General De Cambio Climático, Transitorios Article 2.

37. "Proponen Diputados Ley de Mitigacion a Cambio Climatico," *SDP Noticias*, November 23, 2010; "Mexican President Calderon's Party Promotes Bill to Tax Emissions," *International Trade Reporter*, August 26, 2010.

38. Carlos Cruz Pacheco, "Comprometidos Senadores a Aprobar Ley General de Cambio Climático en Septiembre," May 3, 2011, Argonmexico.com (accessed on May 31, 2011).

5

Conclusions and Policy Recommendations

As this book has detailed, addressing the challenges of climate change has become more difficult and costly for the United States, Canada, and Mexico. Climate policy faces uncertain prospects in all three countries. In each, federal regulations and actions by subnational governments seek to supplement, and often substitute for, national climate policies. The US Environmental Protection Agency (EPA) is pursuing new environmental regulations in the face of an impasse over national climate legislation in Congress. A few US states and Canadian provinces are implementing economy-wide cap-and-trade legislation, and most have renewable energy and energy-efficiency policies in place. The Mexican government has formulated plans to reduce its emissions but will need more funding and capacity assistance from developed countries to fulfill its ambitious goals.

In the preceding chapters, we have explored three major challenges in crafting climate policy. The first is to manage regional economic impacts within countries. In Canada, there is a geographic split between the western provinces, which depend on the oil and gas industry for economic growth, and other provinces that have a diversified industrial base and derive a greater share of power from renewable sources. In the United States, climate action consists of a patchwork of measures pursued by a number of eastern and western states. To generalize broadly, divisions exist between coastal states, some of which are beginning to develop clean technology industries, and inland states that have high endowments of coal, oil, and greenhouse gas (GHG)–intensive manufacturing. In contrast to Canada, where "climate hawkish" and "climate dovish" provinces exist in roughly equal number, US states pursuing serious climate action are the exception rather than the rule.

While most states have some form of renewable portfolio or energy-efficiency standard for utilities, only a handful are considering an economy-wide approach. As we showed in chapters 2 and 3, the states and provinces that have successfully mobilized political momentum toward stringent climate change policies are mostly those that had relatively little carbon-intensive production to begin with. Getting states and provinces that depend on coal, oil, and energy-intensive sectors for economic growth to join a GHG regulatory regime is a more difficult task.

Unlike most emerging economies that are not obligated to set GHG mitigation goals under UN convention,[1] Mexico has a national plan in place that aims to cut emissions in half by 2050. Distributional concerns also complicate Mexican policy but in a somewhat different way than its northern neighbors. Mexican policy has largely been top-down, and the focus is on technology deployment, forestry, and capacity building rather than carbon pricing or other market mechanisms. As in the United States and Canada, determining who pays for these policies is a challenge. Given the fiscal issues discussed in chapter 4, Mexico hopes to tap foreign sources of finance to develop new green energy technologies and to implement GHG mitigation strategies.

The second related challenge is to address competitiveness concerns. In the United States, lawmakers are focused less on how climate policy's compliance costs will adversely affect regional trade and investment, and more on what kind of threat will be posed by emerging markets that are not obligated to pursue similar policies. China and India are at the forefront of their concerns.

In contrast, competitiveness concerns in Canada focus on the United States. Canada exports the vast majority of its energy-intensive products to the United States. Thus the absence of federal climate change legislation in the United States introduces the risk that any serious Canadian policy to regulate GHG emissions could cause Canadian energy-intensive production to simply migrate across the border. This "carbon leakage" could exacerbate the economic dislocation generated by a stringent Canadian climate change regime. The Harper government has seized upon these potential competitiveness impacts as a reason to tie Canadian efforts to US federal policy on climate change.

Canadian officials are just as afraid of certain types of climate change policies as they are of US inaction. In particular, they have responded sharply to US policies that target carbon-intensive transportation fuels. The province of Alberta is heavily dependent on exports of carbon-intensive oil sands fuels to the United States, and Saskatchewan exports a large amount of conventional crude. US implementation of a low-carbon fuel standard, while benefiting the overall international goal of reducing GHG emissions, could prove disruptive to production and investment in Canadian oil, particularly unconventional oil sands projects.

The third challenge is to align energy and transport infrastructure to improve energy efficiency and expand opportunities for renewables and low-

---

1. The Copenhagen Accord obligated non–Annex I countries (minus least developed countries) to undertake "nationally appropriate mitigation actions." China and India have submitted intensity targets that produce questionable emissions reductions relative to business as usual, and few developing countries have committed to absolute emissions reduction targets. See Cline (2010).

carbon fuels. This challenge applies to all three countries. As we highlighted in chapter 4, North America's antiquated electricity grid is ill suited to the task of transporting renewable electricity from areas where it is abundant to areas where it is needed. The current system is also less able to adjust electricity demand to accommodate intermittent renewable sources. Meanwhile, freight transport infrastructure must be updated in order to avoid long waits at the border and encourage more efficient rail, air, and road networks (CEC 2011). The infrastructure needs are especially pronounced in Mexico and may well require external financing—from nascent "green funds" or regional institutions—to support Mexico's ambitious climate goals and enable it to participate in a future North American climate regime.

Climate policymakers will need to show sensitivity to regional impacts and industrial competitiveness in order to successfully enact climate change legislation. We have highlighted a few options for addressing these concerns in the previous chapters. Undoubtedly, border adjustment mechanisms and free allocations of emissions permits to electric utilities or to vulnerable industries will continue to be examined as a viable mechanism. However, the least trade-distorting and most environmentally sound way to protect industries from competitiveness impacts, prevent regional disparities from becoming more pronounced, and promote capacity building is to harmonize regulations through international accords.

Role of Multilateral Negotiations

For the past two decades, multilateral negotiations have sought to construct a global climate compact that would substantially reduce GHG emissions and promote green growth strategies in developing countries through, inter alia, robust networks for offsets and climate finance. A successful agreement that includes emissions reductions from both developed and developing countries would help mitigate competitiveness concerns by leveling the playing field for carbon-intensive industry. In a world where all large emitters enact stringent regulations to reduce GHG emissions, firms would face less incentive to move emissions-intensive production abroad, and thus the risk of carbon leakage would be diminished.[2]

While international negotiations have made some minor progress, they continue to proceed slowly. The key challenge is to balance the priorities of developed countries with those of the major developing countries. Most developing countries, even relatively advanced ones such as Mexico, do not have as much financial and institutional capacity to reduce emissions as developed countries do. Getting these countries to commit to reducing emissions without substantial financial and capacity assistance from developed countries has been a major challenge for climate negotiators. Developing countries are also reluctant to commit to monitoring, reporting, and verification (MRV)

---

2. For a much more thorough discussion of this point, see Houser et al. (2008).

of carbon credits. Meanwhile, developed countries are reluctant to accept an agreement that omits emissions limits or MRV for developing countries for the simple reason that no global regime will "work" without significant GHG reductions by China, Brazil, India, and others.

The past two years of international negotiations have made modest progress toward resolving these tensions. During the Copenhagen negotiations in December 2009, the US delegation brokered a compromise committing $100 billion in assistance from developed countries for climate change mitigation and adaptation in developing countries. In return, major developing country emitters committed to "nationally appropriate mitigation actions."[3]

The Cancún Agreements in December 2010 reaffirmed developing countries' commitment to national mitigation plans and moved countries closer to a proposal for MRV. Developed countries promised to enhance MRV of their financial commitments in return for "international consultation and analysis" of developing country mitigation actions.[4] The latter includes reporting of countries' planned actions as well as a timeline for their implementation and an assessment of their effectiveness. It also includes a registry to match planned mitigation actions with the appropriate finance from developed countries. Countries made progress on climate finance, establishing a Green Climate Fund to administer a portion of the $100 billion promised in Copenhagen. The fund will be governed by a board with equal representation from developed and developing countries, and will be administered by the World Bank. A standing committee of the fund was established to mobilize sources of finance and coordinate MRV of the funds.

As difficult as it has been to obtain pledges that satisfy both developed and developing countries, it will be even more difficult to implement these pledges. One of the biggest concerns going forward is where climate assistance will come from. Both the United States and the European Union provided money toward fast-track climate assistance pledges in fiscal year 2010, but the United States will have considerable trouble mobilizing climate funds in the near future. Although President Obama asked Congress for $1.9 billion in 2011, both houses of Congress are increasingly reluctant to allocate new funds for international climate aid, and the new leadership in the House of Representatives is not inclined to fund general climate change programs.

Role of North America

The role of North American institutions in addressing the global climate mitigation puzzle is twofold. First, North American institutions have a part to play in supplementing international mitigation efforts, especially where

---

3. Copenhagen Accord, Paragraph 5, http://unfccc.int (accessed on June 8, 2011).

4. The Cancún Agreements: Outcome of the Work of the Ad Hoc Working Group on Long-term Cooperative Action under the Convention, Paragraph 63, http://unfccc.int (accessed on June 8, 2011).

financing and MRV are concerned. Indeed, the Cancún Agreements themselves assign some finance and capacity building to bilateral and regional channels. Although the Green Climate Fund is supposed to administer a large portion of mitigation and adaptation assistance, the agreements call for additional bilateral and multilateral sources to supplement this funding. This is especially true in the case of initiatives for reduced emissions from deforestation and degradation, where bilateral and multilateral capacity-building assistance is needed to establish adequate forest monitoring capabilities and national baseline emissions levels in developing countries.

Second, North America–specific issues (such as border infrastructure, renewable standards, and oil sands regulation) often are better dealt with on a regional platform than in separate bilateral arrangements. Given the large amount of oil, gas, and electricity trade among the three countries, it makes sense for North America to coordinate the decarbonization of its energy supply regionally while the three countries continue to pursue a multilateral accord. For example, with regard to carbon sequestration, it would make sense to coordinate mapping of carbon capture and storage (CCS) sites.

In addition, most of North America's actions on climate change are currently conducted on a subnational level. Multilateral negotiations are ill-suited to dealing with these state measures, as individual states by and large do not participate in them. By contrast, trilateral coordination of state actions is feasible, and there is much that can be done to harmonize renewable portfolio standards and regional cap-and-trade regimes. Due to its smaller scale, the regional platform is also better for addressing the various intranational disparities highlighted in previous chapters.

North American leaders have worked together on energy issues for the past decade. During the early 2000s, the North American Energy Working Group produced a series of reports on cross-border electricity regulation, natural gas production, and energy-efficiency standards and labeling. More recently, in 2009, the North American Leaders' Summit (NALS) pledged a number of actions related to clean energy development. The countries agreed to develop a trilateral working plan on climate change and clean energy to be considered at the subsequent NALS meeting, which will take place in 2011. The plan will support, inter alia, the following actions:

- financing mechanisms to support mitigation and adaptation actions, including Mexico's Green Fund;
- comparable approaches to measuring, reporting, and verifying emissions reductions, a prerequisite for any future North American emissions trading regime;
- work to limit gas flaring;
- collaboration on smart grid interoperability standards;
- cooperation on carbon capture and storage projects;
- alignment of national energy-efficiency standards;

- reduction of GHG emissions in the oil and gas and transportation sectors (which account for a large share of GHG emissions in Mexico); and

- cooperation on sustainable forest management, and on methodologies for quantifying and managing programs to reduce emissions in the forest sector.

In particular, the NAFTA leaders floated the idea of a North American carbon capture and storage partnership. Under the proposed initiative, countries would develop a consensus on the methodology to be employed in estimating the CO_2 storage capacity of various North American sinks. With a common methodology in place, the countries would create a North American carbon atlas, where data from different states, provinces, and organizations regarding carbon sources and sinks could be viewed in a common format. The partnership would also foster collaboration on research and development related to CCS.[5]

North American leaders have also engaged in bilateral talks on energy. In February 2009, the United States and Canada launched the Clean Energy Dialogue, which seeks to promote the "development of clean energy technologies to reduce greenhouse gases and combat climate change."[6] The dialogue established working groups on carbon capture and storage, smart grid infrastructure, and clean energy research and development. In April 2009, the United States and Mexico established the Bilateral Framework on Clean Energy and Climate Change, which promises training and infrastructure to promote clean energy technologies.[7] In May 2010, Presidents Obama and Calderón created the Cross-Border Electricity Task Force to promote regional renewable energy markets.

Energy and climate initiatives have also reinvigorated cooperation within NAFTA. During the August 2010 Commission for Environmental Cooperation (CEC) ministerial meeting in Guanajuato, Mexico, EPA administrator Lisa Jackson praised the "open and transparent dialogue" that the three North American environmental ministers shared within the CEC Council— and that contrasted sharply with the disengaged approach of ministers to NAFTA initiatives earlier in the decade.[8] At this meeting, the council resolved to augment collaboration on improving the comparability of GHG emissions

---

5. Joint statement by North American leaders Felipe Calderón, Stephen Harper, and Barack Obama, August 10, 2009, www.whitehouse.gov (accessed on June 8, 2011).

6. White House, President Obama and Prime Minister Harper Vow Joint Effort on North American Economic Recovery, Office of the Press Secretary, February 19, 2009, www.whitehouse.gov (accessed on June 8, 2011).

7. White House, U.S.-Mexico Announce Bilateral Framework on Clean Energy and Climate Change, Office of the Press Secretary, April 16, 2009.

8. Remarks by Lisa Jackson at the welcoming reception for the Commission for Environmental Cooperation Council, Guanajuato, Mexico, August 16, 2010, http://yosemite.epa.gov/opa (accessed on June 8, 2011).

data gathering, methodologies, and inventories and systems; the goal was to share climate change information in order to support GHG reductions in North America via mitigation and adaptation projects. The council also resolved to support various public-private partnerships to encourage the transition to a lower-carbon economy, for example in the area of green building.

Policy Recommendations

The NAFTA leaders have begun to explore areas where North American cooperation on climate change could have value and produce concrete results. To be sure, the political environment is not ripe for ambitious legislation on climate change; there is little political will, except in certain scattered states and provinces, for stringent measures. However, there is a broad range of climate initiatives that could advance in the current political environment and that could promote mitigation of GHGs and adoption of new and greener technologies throughout North America.

NAFTA's work on climate change could be significant, both in reinforcing North American economic integration and promoting sustainable development. To those ends, NAFTA institutions should coordinate, harmonize, and facilitate climate change regulations in the region. A successful North American climate change framework could also propel multilateral talks by creating precedents for North-South cooperation on climate change—precedents that could help inform ongoing international efforts to develop a post-Kyoto regime. The following are our recommendations for near-term, practical steps that the NAFTA countries could take in confronting their interrelated climate change challenges.

Harmonize Energy Regulations

1. Study options for coordinating or integrating evolving carbon regimes, at both the federal and state levels.

During the period when national carbon-trading schemes seemed likely in the United States and Canada, there was some discussion of a trilateral carbon market as a way to ensure a uniform price for GHG emissions and thereby apply the same regulatory burden to energy-intensive industries in all three NAFTA countries. This idea has since lost substantial political backing. Though the US EPA seemingly has the authority to put in place a cap-and-trade system for large GHG emitters, this option would prove politically explosive. Instead, the EPA is likely to embrace more modest energy-efficiency performance standards. Following suit, the Harper government has shelved its own cap-and-trade proposal.

Still, harmonized markets for GHG permits, GHG offset credits, renewable electricity, and renewable electricity credits might be created for firms in states and provinces that participate in regional regulatory regimes such as cap-and-trade and renewable portfolio standards. Streamlined markets for permits and credits would in turn make it easier for firms in jurisdictions that will not adopt climate policy to develop low-carbon technologies and receive money for emissions reductions.

Markets that are relatively easy to access and have low transaction costs could provide a source of revenue to finance Mexico's climate change goals. The sale of carbon offsets or renewable energy toward compliance with US or Canadian standards cannot produce additional emissions reductions for Mexico—in other words, these reductions would be credited toward the United States or Canada, not Mexico, in any trilateral or international climate change regime. However, these reductions could spur additional investment in low-carbon infrastructure and technologies, helping Mexico along the path to reach its climate change targets.

What could be done, particularly at the subfederal level, to integrate carbon and renewable energy markets? Previous chapters have pointed out the value of linking nascent regional cap-and-trade programs such as the Regional Greenhouse Gas Initiative and Western Climate Initiative; of streamlining markets for renewable electricity certificates (RECs) used to comply with state renewable portfolio standards; and of using regional institutions to certify carbon offsets used toward compliance with state and provincial regulations. In these areas, the NAFTA CEC could use its prior experience collecting North American emissions data to play a role in monitoring and reporting emissions reductions.

2. Standardize definitions of renewable energy and coordinate policies.

The United States and Canada share a large volume of cross-border electricity trade; this trade accounts for 6 to 10 percent of Canadian annual generation and up to 37 percent of electricity consumption in certain US border states.[9] Consequently, policies that affect renewable electricity production and consumption in Canadian and US border states necessarily have spillover effects on production and consumption in the neighboring country.

Currently, definitions of renewable energy vary widely among states and provinces, complicating regulation of renewable electricity from across the border. The major differences between US and Canadian regulations lie in the eligibility of hydropower to meet renewable standards. Both sides should make virtue out of necessity and agree on how imported electricity should be credited and certified under renewable portfolio standards, at both the federal and state levels. To the extent feasible, states and provinces should harmonize definitions of renewable electricity in order to stimulate renewable electricity development by increasing the liquidity of REC markets.

3. Improve cross-border transmission capacity between the United States and Mexico and between the United States and Canada.

---

9. See the National Energy Board, Electricity Exports and Imports: Monthly Statistics for December 2009, www.neb-one.gc.ca (accessed on June 9, 2011).

Because US-Mexico electricity transmission is inadequate, the ample wind and solar resources in the Mexican border region—some of the best in the world—aren't being sufficiently exploited and sold to the United States. As we highlighted in chapter 4, additional cross-border transmission would allow firms pursuing renewables projects to take advantage of economies of scale; in fact several firms have already located generation sites along both sides of the border in the hopes of scaling up generation for both markets (Wood 2010).

Additional transmission would allow states to adopt more stringent renewable electricity standards by expanding the base of renewable energy available, thereby lowering the cost of compliance. Because Mexican renewable electricity generators near the border could sell electricity at a premium to meet these standards, the transmission would help make solar and wind power more competitive relative to conventional fuels. Transmission upgrades could thus accelerate the development of renewable infrastructure on both sides of the border.

Both Canada and the United States have examined the possibility of revamping the electric grid so that it can better adapt to real-time fluctuations in electricity demand and supply. Such a smart grid is a crucial component in improving energy efficiency and developing renewable energy. A smart grid can better balance multiple variable sources of electricity and manage demand for electricity, allowing utilities to avoid installing additional capacity to meet peak loads. Smart grid pilot programs already exist in several US cities, as well as the Canadian province of Ontario.

In order to construct a seamless North American smart grid, the United States and Canada need to resolve several issues. Transmission congestion currently presents a problem for both countries and they need to coordinate where new transmission should be placed. From there, states and provinces on both sides of the border need to agree on common regulations for transmission construction and on common interoperability standards once these transmission lines are built.

4. Work together to reduce GHG emissions from the oil sands, and coordinate investment in carbon capture and storage.

The oil sands provide energy security to the United States and Canada, but they continue to produce significantly more GHG emissions than conventional oil despite recent improvements in mining and processing technologies. Both countries require an intelligent strategy to reduce emissions from transport fuels while still ensuring that enough oil is produced to meet short-run demand.

Ultimately, the way to achieve both goals is conservation—and oil conservation measures need to be stepped up soon to shield consumers from price increases that are expected to occur whether the oil sands are developed or not (EIA 2011a). Though Canada bills its oil as "energy-secure," the fact is that under the business-as-usual scenario, rising North American oil demand will increase financial transfers not just to Canada but also to the Middle East and Venezuela. Policies that encourage development of renewable energy and lower-carbon technologies and that promote conservation are much needed and should encompass, inter alia, more stringent fuel efficiency standards and additional investment in low-carbon biofuels.

Though California's low-carbon fuel standard has encountered much criticism in Canada, it could provide an important vehicle to spur investment in alternative fuels. As we pointed out in chapter 2, the standard requires some adjustment to ensure that it does not draw arbitrary distinctions between fuels, violating international trade law. California should consider adding nuance to its life-cycle analysis by separating the basket of "conventional oil" used in California into various categories based on weight, type of extraction, etc. This would make it easier to justify giving oil sands its own separate category, and it would ease concerns that heavy crudes such as those extracted in California are being given special treatment. The downside is that this approach would be more expensive—both administratively and to the California refining industry, whose oil would face a disadvantage compared to lighter, less GHG-intensive fuels.

In addition to investing in alternative fuels, the United States and Canada need to improve methods for carbon sequestration. Substantial research already has been undertaken on CCS, which has the potential to reduce GHGs from oil sands production. If CCS can be successfully commercialized, and if the cost can be lowered sufficiently—both big "ifs"—the technology could benefit both the United States and Canada. CCS deployment, if successful, could help smooth over the regional tensions between GHG reduction and employment in carbon-intensive industries referenced earlier in this chapter and in chapters 2 and 3. It would sharply reduce the GHGs produced from the coal-fired power plants prevalent in many US regions, allowing coal producers to better adapt to climate change legislation and reducing economic dislocation in coal-producing states in the event of stringent GHG regulations. It might also make western Canada's oil-producing provinces more amenable to an ambitious Canadian carbon reduction regime. Toward this end, the United States and Canada should follow through on their commitment to coordinate mapping of sinks and sources for CCS.

At the same time, it is important to have a realistic assessment of the possibilities and limitations of CCS and other technological improvements on the horizon. CCS is not yet fully proven at commercial scale, and it is likely to be exorbitantly expensive when first introduced. Development and commercialization of CCS are at least a decade away, and the cost and feasibility are yet uncertain. In the meantime, the rapid expansion of oil sands production represents a significant source of emissions growth, even as Canada promises to significantly reduce its emissions in the near and medium term. As discussed in chapter 3, the Canadian economy has less low-hanging fruit for emissions reductions than the US economy. It will be difficult for Canada to achieve significant enough emissions reductions from other areas of the economy to compensate for rapid oil sands growth and meet its 2020 Copenhagen targets—to do so would put a strain on non-oil-producing provinces, many of which have large manufacturing sectors.

In the long run, the prospects for the oil sands differ from the prospects for coal; while coal can theoretically be made emissions free, the oil sands cannot. Approximately 70 to 80 percent of the emissions from oil—whether produced from the oil sands or by conventional means—ultimately come from burning the fuel in vehicles rather than in smokestacks, and CCS cannot be applied to mobile sources (NETL 2009). Even assuming successful commercialization of CCS, the problem remains: Over the long term, all three North American countries must sharply reduce consumption of oil in their cars and trucks in order to achieve emissions levels consistent with the need to sharply constrain global warming. New technologies—alternative fuels, electric cars, and fuel efficiency improvements, among others—must slowly replace oil consumption, including consumption of oil sands products. This can occur only as countries adapt to less energy-intensive production and consumption.

Clarify International Trade Law to Avoid New Trade Barriers; Avoid Interpretation of Existing Trade Law in a Way that Would Jeopardize Climate Change Regulations

5. Avoid new trade barriers.

When policymakers craft climate change legislation, they often include provisions that explicitly erect trade barriers for competitiveness reasons or implicitly restrict trade due to specific regulatory requirements. Many are motivated by pressures to prevent domestic industries from moving to unregulated areas where production costs are lower: Border adjustments and subsidies to regulated industries fall into this category. Others, such as the United States' biofuels restrictions and the domestic content requirements of Ontario's Feed-In Tariff, are motivated by the desire to promote domestic firms over foreign competitors.

In the near term, border adjustments should not be used to equalize costs between domestic and foreign producers, as these measures are likely to be emulated or provoke retaliation by other countries. Ideally, World Trade Organization (WTO) rules and climate treaty obligations should address competitiveness concerns in a manner that achieves the environmental objectives without undercutting world trade norms.[10] Without such guidelines, there is likely to be a rash of overzealous litigation or new protectionist measures. Because such a framework would take a few years to develop, the three NAFTA

---

10. Hufbauer, Charnovitz, and Kim (2009) suggest that WTO members negotiate a code of good conduct for trade-related climate change measures and lay out the details of what such a code might look like.

partners should agree to a temporary moratorium on new border measures related to climate change policies. This is particularly necessary in light of current regulatory uncertainty in all three NAFTA countries.

Border adjustments are not the only measures that should be avoided; various types of climate-related subsidies can be trade distorting and would benefit from NAFTA discipline. One category of subsidy is the rebates offered by state and federal cap-and-trade proposals to carbon-intensive industries. In the cap-and-trade regulations in California's Assembly Bill 32, and in previously vetted US cap-and-trade bills such as the American Clean Energy and Security Act, compensation is conveyed in the form of free allowances to firms that are vulnerable to foreign competition and would otherwise face significantly higher production costs under cap-and-trade schemes. The purpose of these subsidies is to prevent these firms from moving to unregulated jurisdictions. Some version of this rebate program may be necessary to allay fears of carbon leakage and obtain political support for future passage of a cap-and-trade program. Nevertheless, if such rebates are needed to cement political support for the climate program, they should be divorced from export performance, to the extent possible, and the amount rebated should not exceed firms' actual costs incurred under the cap-and-trade program.

"Green subsidies" for renewable energy and energy efficiency should be deployed judiciously to spur research but not to pick winners for commercial development. States, provinces, and countries should ensure that these subsidies are targeted to the goal of reducing GHG emissions and do not discriminate based on where the materials used for production originate. Domestic content requirements such as Ontario's could ultimately increase the cost of transitioning to low-carbon energy, because they exclude energy produced using cheaper imported turbines and solar panels. Ontario's feed-in tariff has also produced tension within the world trading system; three countries have litigated this provision in WTO dispute settlement. In order to avoid raising costs and provoking litigation, subsidies should be designed to produce as little trade distortion as possible.

Restrictions on government procurement have inhibited construction of environmental projects in other cases as well. A particularly egregious example is the spate of "Buy American" provisions, which require iron, steel, and manufacturing goods used in construction projects to be produced using 100 percent US-content materials. Recognizing the negative impact of this provision on supply chains that are heavily integrated across the US-Canadian border, the United States and Canada negotiated a supplemental procurement agreement in 2010 that removes significant obstacles facing US and Canadian firms when bidding on public contracts. In essence, the deal provides Canada a waiver on the Buy American provisions in exchange for a lifting of Canadian provincial procurement requirements. However, some provinces have excluded important environmental projects such as public transit infrastructure from the waiver. Meanwhile, the United States limits its Buy American exemptions to procurement by seven programs,[11] and access to US state government procurement contracts applies only to the 37 US states that have signed the WTO Agreement on Government Procurement (Sosnow and Peaker 2010). Going forward, both countries should recognize the importance of US-Canada economic integration to firms participating in government-funded environmental projects, and each country should remove domestic content restrictions for all NAFTA suppliers of publicly financed environmental projects.

As discussed in chapters 2 and 3, domestically produced ethanol is heavily subsidized and protected in both the United States and Canada. The United States currently imposes a 54 cent per gallon tariff on imported ethanol, and Canadian tariffs for non-NAFTA ethanol range between 3 and 6 percent, or about 10 cents per liter. This system of subsidies and tariffs is a lose-lose situation: taxpayers suffer because of the high cost of the subsidies, and the climate suffers because the corn-based ethanol produced in the United States and Canada generates more GHGs than conventional gasoline by some measures.[12] Trade relations with other major ethanol producers such as Brazil are strained by this blatant show of protectionism. Foreign sugarcane-based ethanol production emits much lower levels of GHGs, but high tariffs undercut the competitiveness of these supplies in the US market. Both countries should reduce the tariffs and the subsidies and allow ethanol from sugarcane and other feedstocks to play a larger role in the domestic fuel market.

In sum, the combination of climate change and energy-related trade measures should be avoided where possible. Subsidies, when needed for legitimate environmental purposes, should be narrowly designed with an eye toward minimizing trade frictions. This will help reduce economic distortions and prevent trade disputes from detracting from the overall goal of mitigating climate change.

6. Establish a "safe harbor" to shield climate change taxes and regulations from claims under the indirect takings provisions of NAFTA Chapter 11.

Chapter 11 requires governments to provide compensation to investors for measures that are "tantamount to expropriation." To date, Chapter 11 rulings have deflated excessive expropriation claims filed by NAFTA petitioners seeking redress from environmental laws and regulations. Moreover, when awards were granted, they generally were a small fraction of the amount sought by the claimant.

---

11. These programs are narrowly defined. They include the Department of Agriculture's Water and Waste Disposal Programs and Community Facilities Program, the Department of Energy's Energy Efficiency and Conservation Block Grants and State Energy Program, the Department of Housing and Urban Development's Community Development Block Grants and Public Housing Capital Fund, and the EPA's Clean Water and Drinking Water State Revolving Funds.

12. Nobel laureate Paul Crutzen and coauthors (2008) have argued that corn-based ethanol produces more carbon when land use changes are taken into account, as corn grown for ethanol displaces food crops.

But past experience is not necessarily instructive for prospective cases targeting climate policies. Climate change laws and regulations will most likely have much broader economic effects than prior environmental legislation, and the scope of potential claims under NAFTA Chapter 11 due to climate change laws and regulations could be orders of magnitude greater than the scope of claims filed in the past. The potential for such Chapter 11 litigation against climate change laws could both slow the implementation of measures designed to mitigate GHG emissions and adversely affect flows of trade and investment in the region.

To prevent this outcome, the three NAFTA countries should clarify the definition of expropriation under Chapter 11 to exclude good-faith efforts to combat climate change. Efforts that should be permissible include taxes levied on firms' GHG emissions output, regulations requiring firms to achieve a certain level of emissions reductions, and regulations requiring firms to use best-practice technologies. These taxes and regulations should not be arbitrary and should be subject to appropriate public review processes. This compromise would allow states, provinces, and federal governments to pursue climate objectives without regulatory chill and would avoid lengthy and costly litigation that could delay needed environmental projects.

Use NAFTA Institutions to Support Individual Climate Actions

7. Use NAFTA institutions to support Mexico's climate change plans.

The North American Development Bank (NADB) and Border Environment Cooperation Commission (BECC), two interrelated institutions that fund environmental projects on the US-Mexico border, should provide financial and technical assistance for energy-saving and pollution control projects in support of Mexico's ambitious climate change policies. The NADB has a capital base of $3 billion, but its track record has been spotty (Hufbauer and Schott 2005). At the outset, NADB lending was constrained due to high interest rates, a cumbersome application process, and a focus on wastewater treatment projects to the exclusion of other worthy environmental investments. Over the past decade, however, the NADB/BECC procedures have improved substantially; as a result, the portfolio of subsidized loans has grown markedly (Kass and McCarroll 2008). The cumulative amount of the loans contracted has increased twentyfold in the past decade, from $24 million in 2001 to $570 million in 2011. The total amount of funding under NADB grants increased from $350 million to $650 million in the same time period.[13]

While the scope of the NADB/BECC has officially expanded to include renewable energy and energy efficiency, these projects still make up a tiny portion of the institutions' overall lending portfolio; the BECC has certified

---

13. North American Development Bank, Annual Report: April 1, 2002–March 31, 2003 and Quarterly Status Report: March 31, 2011, San Antonio.

only 3 clean energy projects out of 177 projects to date.[14] Current climate-related projects include a $3 million loan for biodiesel and a $60 million solar loan. The NADB could substantially increase loans to these types of projects without cutting very much into its capital base.

NAFTA facilitation of carbon offset sales from Mexico, as described in the first recommendation above, could also generate revenue that could be put toward climate change measures. Carbon offsets do not necessarily substitute for outside climate assistance, as they provide no additionality—Mexican emissions reductions financed by carbon offsets would otherwise occur in the jurisdiction imposing the regulations with which the offsets are used to comply. In the absence of additional financing, however, they might serve as a way to build infrastructure for low-carbon development and to incentivize fledgling companies to enter markets for clean energy and transport vehicles.

8. Use the Commission for Environmental Cooperation as a clearinghouse for climate change–related data.

The CEC discussed responses to climate change in the mid-1990s but failed to take concrete action. Subsequently, NAFTA officials put climate change on ice. Since 2009, however, the issue has gained salience on the NAFTA agenda. North American environmental ministers now regard the CEC as a useful forum for trilateral cooperation on the nexus of energy and environmental issues that are crucial to the achievement of each country's climate policy goals.

To date, the CEC has been plagued by a broad mandate and a narrow financial base. Its charge is to amass environmental information, provide recommendations on trilateral environmental issues, and promote environmental law enforcement—all on a $9 million annual budget.[15] Although the CEC has been effective for its size, its budget constrains the scope and effectiveness of its operations (Hufbauer and Schott 2005).

The CEC should focus its resources on a few issues of primary importance, and climate change is a natural candidate for that list, given the magnitude of the problem and its significance to the future of the North American economy. The CEC's climate agenda should be targeted at initiatives that help inform policy implementation in each country. Its comparative advantage lies in its capacity to amass information from a number of different sources and consolidate it into a product that is useful across jurisdictions (Craik 2010). A prime example is its North American Pollutant Release and Transfer Register (NAPRTR) program, which collects toxics data from the three North American countries and inputs them into a standardized, firm-level database. The NAPRTR program has successfully raised awareness of environ-

---

14. North American Development Bank, Quarterly Status Report: March 31, 2011, San Antonio.

15. The amount of money allocated to the CEC has remained unchanged since its creation in 1994, despite inflation and exchange rate movements (the budget is expressed in dollars, while the CEC is located in Montreal and incurs most of its expenses in Canadian dollars) that have decreased the real value of this amount. See Hufbauer and Schott (2005).

mental challenges. Not only has it enhanced the accessibility of environmental reporting, but it has enhanced the reporting itself; the NAPRTR program led and supported Mexico in developing its own pollution tracking registry.

With modest budgetary increases, the CEC could play a similar role in NAFTA climate change initiatives and become a clearinghouse for data on all North American emissions, including GHGs. All three countries have GHG emissions inventories, even though not all of them include GHGs in the data sets that they report to the CEC. Collecting, consolidating, and mapping these data should be part of the CEC's domain. The CEC has already incorporated this goal into its strategic objectives for 2015 and has begun laying the groundwork for a project in this vein.[16]

By making detailed GHG emissions information easily available across the three North American countries, the CEC could facilitate monitoring, reporting, and verification of carbon credits issued under national or regional carbon regimes. Facilitating MRV could in turn lower transaction costs for offset projects among the three countries and increase the credibility of national inventories, thus supporting fungibility and the integrity of possible offset investments in Mexico and elsewhere. These results could be a boon for low-carbon development in states and provinces that do not immediately choose to join regional efforts to reduce GHG emissions. They could also facilitate low-carbon development in Mexico.

The CEC should also report on new climate initiatives and regulations in each country. A single, harmonized database of climate change laws and regulations could assist trilateral collaboration by highlighting areas of synergy and tension among the three countries' policies. Such a database would fit well into the CEC's current work plan; a draft 2011–12 project proposal recommends that the CEC create an online platform to enable North American government officials to share data related to climate change.[17]

Summing Up

Broadly, North American climate and energy policy must accomplish three goals to be successful. First, it must reduce GHG emissions—and not simply displace those emissions elsewhere. The threat of carbon leakage provides a disincentive for states and provinces with energy-intensive industries—precisely those that most need to reduce emissions—from pursuing adaptation and mitigation strategies.

Second, it must ensure that the cost of reducing emissions is manageable; only in this way will it encourage adaptation and avoid a political backlash.

16. Commission for Environmental Cooperation, Project 2: Improving Comparability of GHG Emissions Data, Methodologies and Inventories in North America, www.cec.org (accessed on May 8, 2011).

17. Commission for Environmental Cooperation, Project 11: North American On-line, Interactive Informational Platform on Climate Change (draft), www.cec.org (accessed on May 8, 2011).

Reducing GHGs will require changes in the way firms and individuals produce and consume goods. Production and consumption must use cleaner forms of energy and become more energy efficient. NAFTA policymakers will face strong resistance to climate programs unless they can ease the transition by reducing and spreading out over time the costs to consumers and local industries. The transition to a lower-carbon economy could be undercut if high economic costs encourage policymakers to compensate consumers and industries by providing subsidies that dampen incentives to conserve or adopt new low-carbon energy technologies.

Third, it must equitably distribute costs so that they are shared across different regions of the continent. Legislative politics requires appeasement of local constituencies; skewed distribution of the compliance costs would complicate the task of securing political support from politicians representing the losing regions. Failure to balance the costs could also lead politicians from the losing regions to seek exemptions from the rules of the climate regime in order to lessen the impact on their constituents. Such an outcome would ultimately reduce the effectiveness of climate policy and increase costs for the entire economy.

At the outset of this chapter, we revisited some of the challenges faced in meeting these goals. In order to contribute to global emissions reductions, policymakers must grapple with both the real and perceived tendency for taxes and regulations to cause emissions to migrate over the border into unregulated jurisdictions. They must deal with wide differences in energy consumption and production patterns. The United States and Canada must bring Mexico into a trilateral regulatory regime. And the infrastructural deficit must be remedied so that clean energy can find its way from the areas that are best for producing it to areas that need to consume it.

To address these challenges, North America eventually needs an integrated carbon market. A large, integrated market would confer significant economic benefits that would allow all three countries to achieve the goals stated above. Greater uniformity of regulations would prevent GHG-intensive firms from moving to or selling to unregulated jurisdictions in order to escape climate-related standards. An integrated carbon market would produce efficiency gains by allowing firms to find the cheapest GHG reductions available in North America. As we pointed out earlier in the book, this could be especially important to Canada, where the cost of cap-and-trade is expected to be significantly higher without policy harmonization and market linkage with the United States. Finally, a large market would provide liquidity, reducing price volatility.

Our recommendations will not create this carbon market, but they do lay the groundwork for coordinating future action toward that end. By using North American institutions to reduce the transaction costs of trading emissions credits, North American countries can encourage states, provinces, and individual firms to participate in nascent state and local regimes. Although state and provincial carbon and renewable electricity markets represent only a portion of total North American emissions, harmonization of these local regulations, to the extent possible, would also be a move toward an integrated North American carbon regime. Investment in transmission infrastructure along the US-Mexico and US-Canada borders would afford renewable electricity a wider customer base and allow generators to take advantage of renewable electricity premiums in other jurisdictions.

To provide a stable, predictable regulatory environment and prevent costly litigation, countries need to clarify certain provisions of international trade law, including Chapter 11 and codes regarding border adjustments and climate subsidies. Litigation reduces regulatory certainty, making firms more reluctant to make the investments needed to comply with regulations. Consistent, clear rules can prevent abuses of international trade law while offering policy predictability to firms and jurisdictions that follow the rules. Meanwhile, avoiding new trade barriers will help preserve the open energy market that North America depends on.

Our recommendations provide a way for individual North American countries to adopt policies to achieve climate goals. Even if these recommendations are acted on, passing climate legislation remains an uphill battle in all three countries. By taking steps to smooth out regional tensions and by providing a framework for an integrated market, however, North American countries can make it easier to pass climate bills in the future and can make the bills eventually enacted more effective.

Climate change policy surely poses challenges for trade and investment in North America, but the problem of climate change also presents an opportunity to deepen ties among the three North American countries. While areas of tension do exist, there are numerous synergies to be exploited. Ultimately, the NAFTA partners share the same priorities: energy security, climate change mitigation, and economic growth. The United States, Canada, and Mexico should build on these common goals to build a foundation for a prosperous future.

References

Alix-Garcia, Jennifer, Alain de Janvry, Elisabeth Sadoulet, and Juan Manuel Torres. 2005. An Assessment of Mexico's Payment for Environmental Services Program. Prepared for the UN Food and Agriculture Organization. Available at http://are.berkeley.edu/~sadoulet (accessed on June 3, 2011).

Auld, Douglas. 2008. *The Ethanol Trap: Why Policies to Promote Ethanol as Fuel Need Rethinking*. C. D. Howe Institute Commentary no. 268. Toronto: C. D. Howe Institute.

Bataille, Chris, Michael Wolinetz, Jotham Peters, Michelle Bennett, and Nic Rivers. 2009. *Exploration of Two Canadian Greenhouse Gas Emissions Targets: 25% below 1990 and 20% below 2006 Levels by 2020*. Vancouver, BC: M. K. Jaccard and Associates. Available at http://pubs.pembina.org (accessed on May 8, 2011).

BCMEM (British Columbia Ministry of Energy and Mines). 2010. *Feed-In Tariff Regulation*. Consultation Paper. Available at www.empr.gov.bc.ca (accessed on May 8, 2011).

BCMOE (British Columbia Ministry of the Environment). 2010. *Emissions Trading Regulation*. Consultation Paper. Available at www.env.gov.bc.ca (accessed on May 8, 2011).

Bianco, Nicholas, and Franz Litz. 2010. *Reducing Greenhouse Gas Emissions in the United States Using Existing Federal Authorities and State Action*. Washington: World Resources Institute.

Blake, Cassels and Graydon, LLP. 2008. Overview of Electricity Regulation in Canada. Available at www.blakes.com (accessed on February 17, 2010).

Boyce, James, and Matthew Riddle. 2009. *Cap and Dividend: A State-by-State Analysis*. Amherst, MA: Political Economy Research Institute, University of Massachusetts, Amherst.

Burtraw, Dallas, Arthur Fraas, and Nathan Richardson. 2011. *Greenhouse Gas Regulation under the Clean Air Act: A Guide for Economists*. RFF Discussion Paper 11-8. Washington: Resources for the Future.

Burtraw, Dallas, Richard Sweeney, and Margaret A. Walls. 2008. *The Incidence of US Climate Policy: Where You Stand Depends on Where You Sit*. Washington: Resources for the Future.

Burtraw, Dallas, Margaret Walls, and Joshua Blonz. 2009. *Distributional Impacts of Carbon Pricing Policies in the Electricity Sector*. RFF Discussion Paper 09-43. Washington: Resources for the Future.

Bushnell, James, Carla Peterman, and Catherine Wolfram. 2007. *Local Solutions to Global Problems: Policy Choice and Regulatory Jurisdiction.* NBER Working Paper 13472. Cambridge, MA: National Bureau of Economic Research. Available at http://www.nber.org/papers/w13472.pdf (accessed on November 12, 2008).

Canadian Council of Chief Executives. 2010. *Clean Growth 2.0: How Canada Can Be a Leader in Energy and Environmental Innovation.* Available at http://ceocouncil.ca (accessed on May 18, 2011).

CARB (California Air Resources Board). 2009. *Detailed CA-GREET Pathway for California Reformulated Gasoline Blendstock for Oxygenate Blending (CARBOB) from Average Crude Refined in California.* Available at www.arb.ca.gov (accessed on May 21, 2011).

CARB (California Air Resources Board). 2010a. *Proposed Regulation to Implement the California Cap-and-Trade Program: Appendix J: Allowance Allocation.* Available at www.arb.ca.gov (accessed on May 21, 2011).

CARB (California Air Resources Board). 2010b. *Proposed Regulation to Implement the California Cap-and-Trade Program: Appendix K: Leakage Analysis.* Available at www.arb.ca.gov (accessed on May 21, 2011).

CBO (Congressional Budget Office). 2009. *Cost Estimate: H.R. 2454, American Clean Energy and Security Act of 2009.* Washington.

CEC (Commission for Environmental Cooperation). 1995. *Council Resolution #95-6: Statement of Intent to Cooperate on Climate Change and Joint Implementation.* Oaxaca, Mexico, October 13. Available at www.cec.org (accessed on June 8, 2011).

CEC (Commission for Environmental Cooperation). 2007. *Fostering Renewable Energy Markets in North America.* Montreal: Commission for Environmental Cooperation.

CEC (Commission for Environmental Cooperation). 2010. *Ministerial Statement.* Seventeenth Regular Session of the CEC Council. Available at www.cec.org (accessed on June 8, 2011).

CEC (Commission for Environmental Cooperation). 2011. *Destination Sustainability: Reducing GHG Emissions from Freight Transportation in North America.* Montreal: Commission for Environmental Cooperation.

Centro Mario Molina. 2008. Low Carbon Growth: A Potential Path for Mexico. Discussion draft presented at United Nations Climate Change Conference (COP-14), Poznan, Poland, December 1–8.

Chen, Cliff, Ryan Wiser, and Mark Bolinger. 2007. *Weighing the Costs and Benefits of Renewables Portfolio Standards: A Comparative Analysis of State-Level Policy Impact Projections.* Berkeley: Lawrence Berkeley National Laboratory. Available at http://eetd.lbl.gov (accessed on May 1, 2009).

Cline, William. 2010. US Climate Change Policy: Implementing Copenhagen and Beyond. Paper presented at the conference "The Transatlantic Relationship in an Era of Growing Economic Multipolarity" held at the Peterson Institute for International Economics, October 8.

Craik, Neil. 2010. Regional Climate Policy Facilitation: The Role of the Commission on Environmental Cooperation. Paper presented at Designing Integration: Regional Governance on Climate Change in North America, Waterloo, Ontario, September 16.

Credit Suisse. 2010. *Growth from Subtraction: Impact of EPA Rules on Power Markets.* London: Credit Suisse.

Creech, Dennis, Eliot Metzger, Samantha Putt del Pino, and John D. Wilson. 2009. *Southeast Energy Opportunities: Local Clean Power.* Washington: World Resources Institute.

Crutzen, P. J., A. R. Mosier, K. A. Smith, and W. Winiwarter. 2008. N2O Release from Agro-Biofuel Production Negates Global Warming Reduction by Replacing Fossil Fuels. *Atmospheric Chemistry and Physics* 8 (August): 389–95.

Dachis, Benjamin. 2009. A Clean Canada in a Dirty World: The Cost of Climate-Related Border Measures. C. D. Howe E-Brief no. 90, C. D. Howe Institute. Available at www.cdhowe.org (accessed on May 18, 2011).

Davis, Lucas. 2008. The Effect of Driving Restrictions on Air Quality in Mexico City. *Journal of Political Economy* 116 (1): 38–81.

Davis, Lucas, and Matthew Kahn. 2008. *International Trade in Used Durable Goods: The Environmental Consequences of NAFTA*. NBER Working Paper 14565. Cambridge, MA: National Bureau of Economic Research.

DOE (Department of Energy). 2008. *20 Percent Wind Energy by 2030: Increasing Wind Energy's Contribution to U.S. Electricity Supply*. Available at www1.eere.energy.gov (accessed on June 7, 2011).

Dworsky, Michael, Marc A. C. Hafstead, and Lawrence H. Goulder. 2009. *Profit Impacts of Allowance Allocation under the American Clean Energy and Security (ACES) Act*. Available at www-siepr.stanford.edu (accessed on May 21, 2009).

EIA (Energy Information Administration). 2003. Greenhouse Gas Emissions, Allowances, Offsets and Commitments of Developing Countries. In *Analysis of S. 139, The Climate Stewardship Act of 2003*. Washington.

EIA (Energy Information Administration). 2008. *Energy Independence and Security Act of 2007: Summary of Provisions*. Available at www.eia.doe.gov (accessed on July 14, 2009).

EIA (Energy Information Administration). 2009. *Mexico Background Note*. Available at www.eia.doe.gov (accessed on March 11, 2010).

EIA (Energy Information Administration). 2010. *International Energy Outlook 2010*. Available at www.eia.gov/oiaf/ieo (accessed May 30, 2011).

EIA (Energy Information Administration). 2011a. *Annual Energy Outlook 2011*. Available at www.eia.gov (accessed on May 30, 2011).

EIA (Energy Information Administration). 2011b. *Oil Overview*. Available at www.eia.doe.gov (accessed on May 6, 2011).

Environment Canada. 2006. *Notice of Intent to Develop a Federal Regulation Requiring Renewable Fuels*. Available at http://gazette.gc.ca (accessed on February 19, 2010).

Environment Canada. 2008a. *Canada National Inventory Report*. Available at www.ec.gc.ca (accessed on June 8, 2011).

Environment Canada. 2008b. *Turning the Corner: Canada's Energy and GHG Emissions Projections: Reference Case: 2006–2020: Provincial and Territorial Tables*. Ottawa.

Environment Canada. 2010. *National Inventory Report 1990–2008: Greenhouse Gas Sources and Sinks in Canada*. Available at www.ec.gc.ca/ges-ghg (accessed on June 4, 2011).

EPA (Environmental Protection Agency). 2009. *Waxman-Markey Discussion Draft Preliminary Analysis: EPA Preliminary Analysis of the American Clean Energy and Security Act of 2009*. Available at www.epa.gov (accessed on May 30, 2011).

EPA (Environmental Protection Agency), US International Trade Commission, Department of Energy, US Treasury, Department of Commerce, and Energy Information Administration. 2009. *The Effects of H.R. 2454 on International Competitiveness and Emission Leakage in Energy-Intensive Trade-Exposed Industries: An Interagency Report Responding to a Request from Senators Bayh, Specter, Stabenow, McCaskill, and Brown*. Washington.

ESMAP (Energy Sector Management Assistance Program). 2004. *Energy Policies and the Mexican Economy*. Washington: World Bank.

Ezekiel, Ron, and Paul Wilson. 2008. *British Columbia Tables Greenhouse Gas Cap and Trade Legislation*. Fasken Martineau, Energy and Environmental Law Bulletin. Available at www.fasken.com/ (accessed on May 21, 2011).

Fickling, Meera. 2010. *North American Climate Change Legislation by State and Province*. Washington: Peterson Institute for International Economics.

Fox, Glenn, and Kenneth Shwedel. 2007. *North American Ethanol Bioenergy Policies and Their NAFTA Implications*. Available at http://naamic.tamu.edu (accessed on November 10, 2009).

Garrison, John. 2010. *Clean Energy & Climate Change Opportunities: Assessment for USAID/Mexico.* Washington: US Agency for International Development.

Garten Rothkopf. 2009. *A Blueprint for Green Energy in the Americas.* Volume 2. Washington: Garten Rothkopf.

Gittell, Ross, and Matt Magnusson. 2008. *Economic Impact in New Hampshire of the Regional Greenhouse Gas Initiative (RGGI): An Independent Assessment.* Durham, NH: University of New Hampshire Whittemore School of Business and Economics.

Government of Alberta. 2010. *Energizing Investment: A Framework to Improve Alberta's Natural Gas and Conventional Oil Competitiveness.* Calgary.

Government of Canada. 2000. *Action Plan 2000 on Climate Change.* Available at www.nrcan.gc.ca (accessed on June 9, 2011).

Gruetter, Juerg. 2007. The CDM in the Transport Sector. In *Sustainable Transport: A Sourcebook for Policy-makers in Developing Cities,* ed. Deutsche Gesellschaft für Technische Zusammenarbeit.

Gruetter, Juerg. 2011. Improvement of Methodologies for Mass Rapid Transport Systems. Presentation at Improvement of CDM Methodologies for Transportation, UNFCCC Practitioners' Workshop, Bonn, Germany, March 3.

Hassett, Kevin A., Aparna Mathur, and Gilbert E. Metcalf. 2008. *The Incidence of a U.S. Carbon Tax: A Lifetime and Regional Analysis.* AEI Working Paper no. 141. Washington: American Enterprise Institute.

Ho, Mun, Richard Morgenstern, and Jhih-Shyang Shih. 2008. *Impact of Carbon Price Policies on US Industry.* Washington: Resources for the Future.

Holt, Edward, and Ryan Wiser. 2007. *The Treatment of Renewable Energy Certificates, Emissions Allowances, and Green Power Programs in State Renewables Portfolio Standards.* Berkeley: Lawrence Berkeley National Laboratory.

Horlick, Gary, Christiane Schuchhardt, and Howard Mann. 2002. *NAFTA Provisions and the Electricity Sector.* Background Paper to the Secretariat Report to the Council, North American Commission for Environmental Cooperation (CEC). Montreal: CEC.

Houser, Trevor, Rob Bradley, Britt Childs, Jacob Werksman, and Robert Heilmayr. 2008. *Leveling the Carbon Playing Field.* Washington: Peterson Institute for International Economics and World Resources Institute.

Howse, Robert, and Petrus van Bork. 2005. Opportunities and Barriers for Renewable Energy in NAFTA. Paper presented at the Third North American Symposium on Assessing the Environmental Effects of Trade, North American Commission for Environmental Cooperation, Montreal, November 30-December 1.

Huacuz, Jorge M. 2007. *The Current Status of Renewable Energy in Mexico.* Cuernavaca: Electrical Research Institute.

Hufbauer, Gary C., and Jisun Kim. 2009. *U.S. Climate Change Legislation and Prospects: Challenges for Canada.* Ottawa: Conference Board of Canada. Available at www.conferenceboard.ca (accessed on May 18, 2011).

Hufbauer, Gary C., and Jeffrey J. Schott. 2005. *NAFTA Revisited: Achievements and Challenges.* Washington: Institute for International Economics.

Hufbauer, Gary, Steve Charnovitz, and Jisun Kim. 2009. *Global Warming and the World Trading System.* Washington: Peterson Institute for International Economics.

Hufbauer, Gary C., Daniel C. Esty, Diana Orejas, Luis Rubio, and Jeffrey J. Schott. 2000. *NAFTA and the Environment: Seven Years Later.* Policy Analyses in International Economics 61. Washington: Institute for International Economics.

ICCC (Intersecretarial Commission on Climate Change). 2007. *National Strategy on Climate Change.* Mexico City: Semarnat.

ICCC (Intersecretarial Commission on Climate Change). 2009. *Special Program on Climate Change 2009–2012*. Mexico City: Semarnat.

IEA (International Energy Agency). 2008. CO_2 Emissions from Fuel Combustion 1971-2006.

IHS CERA. 2010. *Oil Sands, Greenhouse Gases, and US Oil Supply: Getting the Numbers Right*. Cambridge.

IHS CERA. 2011. *Oil Sands Technology: Past, Present and Future*. Cambridge.

Johnson, Todd, Claudio Alatorre, Zayra Romo, and Feng Liu. 2010. *Low Carbon Development for Mexico*. Washington: World Bank.

Karousakis, Katia. 2007. *Incentives to Reduce GHG Emissions from Deforestation: Lessons Learned from Costa Rica and Mexico*. Environment Directorate, International Energy Agency. Paris: International Energy Agency.

Komives, Kristin, Todd Johnson, Jonathan Halpern, Jose Luis Aburto, and John Scott. 2009. *Residential Electricity Subsidies in Mexico*. Washington: World Bank.

Kass, Stephen L., and Jean McCarroll. 2008. Environmental Enforcement and Protection under NAFTA. *New York Law Journal*. Available at www.clm.com (accessed on May 8, 2011).

Laan, Tara, Todd Alexander Litman, and Ronald Steenblik. 2009. *Biofuels—At What Cost: Government Support for Ethanol and Biodiesel in Canada*. Winnipeg: International Institute for Sustainable Development.

Lokey, Elizabeth. 2008. Barriers to Clean Development Mechanism Renewable Energy Projects in Mexico. *Renewable Energy* 34: 504–08.

Manitoba Conservation. 2011. *Public Consultation on a Proposed Cap and Trade System for Manitoba*. Winnipeg.

Maruyama, Warren. 2010. Trade and WTO Aspects of U.S. Climate Change Legislation: Cap–and–Trade or Carbon Tax? Draft paper prepared for the Fair Trade Center. Hogan and Hartson LLP.

Mata, Juan. 2006. Mexico: Large-Scale Renewable Energy Development Project. Presentation at Energy Week conference, Washington, March 8.

McKibben, Warwick, and Peter J. Wilcoxen. 2009. *The Economic and Environmental Effects of Border Tax Adjustments for Climate Policy*. Lowy Institute Working Paper 1.09. Sydney: Lowy Institute.

McKinsey and Company. 2008. *Carbon Capture and Storage: Assessing the Economics*. Available at www.mckinsey.com (accessed on July 14, 2009).

Mexico City (Mexico City Secretary of the Environment). 2008. *Programa de Acción Climática de la Ciudad de Mexico 2008–2012*. Mexico City.

Monast, Jonas, Tim Profeta, and David Cooley. 2010. *Avoiding the Glorious Mess: A Sensible Approach to Climate Change and the Clean Air Act*. Nicholas Institute Working Paper. Available at http://nicholasinstitute.duke.edu (accessed on June 3, 2011).

Morgenstern, Richard, and Eric Moore. 2010. *California Industry Impacts of a Statewide Carbon Pricing Policy*. Washington: Resources for the Future.

NETL (National Energy Technology Laboratory). 2009. *An Evaluation of the Extraction, Transport and Refining of Imported Crude Oils and the Impact of Life Cycle Greenhouse Gas Emissions*. DOE/NETL-2009/1362. Washington: Department of Energy.

Nova Scotia DOE (Nova Scotia Department of Energy). 2010. *Renewable Energy in Nova Scotia: Feed-In Tariff*. Available at www.nsrenewables.ca (accessed on May 8, 2011).

NRTEE (National Roundtable on the Environment and the Economy). 2009. *Achieving 2050: A Carbon Pricing Policy for Canada*. Ottawa: NRTEE. Available at www.nrtee-trnee.com (accessed on May 18, 2011).

NRTEE (National Roundtable on the Environment and the Economy). 2011. *Parallel Paths: Canada-US Policy Choices*. Ottawa.

Ontario MOE (Ontario Ministry of the Environment). 2009. *Moving Forward: A Greenhouse Gas Cap-and-Trade System for Ontario*. Available at www.ene.gov.on.ca (accessed on February 18, 2010).

Paul, Anthony, Dallas Burtraw, and Karen Palmer. 2008. *Compensation for Electricity Consumers under a US CO2 Emissions Cap*. RFF Discussion Paper 08-25. Washington: Resources for the Future.

Peters, Jotham, Chris Bataille, Nic Rivers, and Marc Jaccard. 2010. *Taxing Emissions, Not Income: How to Moderate the Regional Impact of Federal Environment Policy*. C. D. Howe Commentary 314. Toronto: C. D. Howe Institute.

Point Carbon. 2010. *Plan B—Going It Alone: Regional Programs in North America*. Washington: Point Carbon.

Powell, Sarah, and James Reid. 2010. Canada: Japan Challenges Ontario's Renewable Energy FIT Program. In *Mondaq Energy and Natural Resources Newsletter*. Available at www.mondaq.com (accessed on May 8, 2011).

Pugua, Nicolas. 2007. Recent Developments in US-Mexico Electricity Trade: A Tale of Two Borders. Presentation at the Border Energy Forum, San Diego, October 18–19.

Rabe, Barry. 1999. Federalism and Entrepreneurship: Explaining American and Canadian Innovation in Pollution Prevention and Regulatory Integration. *Policy Studies Journal* 27(2): 288–306.

Rabe, Barry. 2006. *Race to the Top: The Expanding Role of U.S. State Renewable Portfolio Standards*. Washington: Pew Center on Global Climate Change.

RGGI (Regional Greenhouse Gas Initiative). 2008. *Regional Greenhouse Gas Initiative Model Rule*. Available at www.rggi.org (accessed on June 10, 2011).

RGGI Emissions Leakage Multi-State Staff Working Group. 2007. *Potential Emissions Leakage and the Regional Greenhouse Gas Initiative (RGGI): Evaluating Market Dynamics, Monitoring Options, and Possible Mitigation Mechanisms*. Available at www.rggi.org (accessed on June 7, 2011).

Richardson, Nathan. 2010. *International Greenhouse Gas Offsets under the Clean Air Act*. RFF Discussion Paper 10-24. Washington: Resources for the Future. Available at www.rff.org (accessed on June 3, 2011).

Richardson, Nathan, Arthur Fraas, and Dallas Burtraw. 2010. *Greenhouse Gas Regulation under the Clean Air Act: Structure, Effects, and Implications of a Knowable Pathway*. RFF Discussion Paper 10-23. Washington: Resources for the Future. Available at www.rff.org (accessed on June 3, 2011).

Roland-Holst, David. 2010. *Real Incomes, Employment, and California Climate Policy*. Research Paper 1004271. Berkeley: Center for Energy, Resources, and Economic Sustainability, University of California, Berkeley.

Rose, Adam, Dan Wei, and Fynnwin Prager. 2010. *Impacts of Climate Policy on the California Economy*. Available at www.next10.org (accessed on June 10, 2011).

Rowlands, Ian H. 2009. Renewable Electricity Politics Across Borders. In *Changing Climates in North American Politics: Institutions, Policymaking, and Multilevel Governance*, ed. Henrik Selin and Stacy VanDeveer. Cambridge, MA: MIT Press.

Sawyer, Dave, and Carolyn Fischer. 2010. *Better Together? The Implications of Linking Canada-US Greenhouse Gas Policies*. C. D. Howe Institute Commentary no. 307. Toronto: C. D. Howe Institute.

Searchinger, Timothy. 2008. Use of U.S. Croplands for Biofuels Increases Greenhouse Gases Through Emissions from Land-Use Change. *Science* 319, no. 5867 (February): 1238–40.

Selin, Henrik, and Stacy D. VanDeveer. 2009. *Changing Climates in North American Politics: Institutions, Policymaking, and Multilevel Governance*. Cambridge, MA: Massachusetts Institute of Technology.

SENER. (Secretary of Energy). 2007. *Programa Sectorial de Energía, 2007–12*. Mexico City.

SENER (Secretary of Energy). 2009. *National Program for Sustainable Use of Energy*. Mexico City.

Serra, Juan Carlos. 2009. Oil and Gas in Mexico: Recent Amendments in the Energy Sector. *Energy Law Advisor* 3, no. 1 (March).

Sosnow, Cliff, and David Peaker. 2010. *The "Buy American" Agreement: Opening Up the Canadian and U.S. Procurement Markets.* Blakes, Cassels, and Graydon LLP. Available at www.blakes.com (accessed on May 24, 2011).

Statistics Canada. 2009. *Electric Power Generation, Transmission, and Distribution.* Available at www.statcan.gc.ca (accessed on June 10, 2011).

Statistics Canada, 2010a. *Energy Statistics Handbook.* Available at www.statcan.gc.ca (accessed on June 8, 2011).

Statistics Canada. 2010b. *Population by Year, by Province, and by Territory.* Available at www40.statcan.gc.ca (accessed on May 6, 2011).

Toman, Michael, Aimee E. Curtright, David S. Ortiz, Joel Darmstadter, and Brian Shannon. 2008. *Unconventional Fossil-Based Fuels: Economic and Environmental Trade-Offs.* Santa Monica: RAND Corporation.

Torres Landa, Juan Francisco, and Mario Jorge Yanez Vega. 2011. Mexico. In *The International Comparative Legal Guide to Environment and Climate Change 2011.* London: Global Legal Group.

Tudela, Fernando. 2003. Institutional Capacity for Climate Change Mitigation in Mexico. In *Institutional Capacity and Climate Actions.* Paris: Organization for Economic Cooperation and Development. Available at www.oecd.org (accessed on March 29, 2010).

UNFCCC (UN Framework Convention on Climate Change). 2010a. *Mexico: National Mitigation Actions Submitted to the Copenhagen Accord.* Available at http://unfccc.int (accessed on May 6, 2011).

UNFCCC (UN Framework Convention on Climate Change). 2010b. *Submission of Canada to the Copenhagen Accord.* Available at http://unfccc.int (accessed on May 8, 2011).

USAID (US Agency for International Development). 2009. *Análisis Comparativo del Marco Eléctrico Legal y Regulatorio de EE. UU. y México para la Promoción de la Energía Eólica.* Washington.

USCAP (US Climate Action Partnership). 2009. *A Call for Action.* Available at www.us-cap.org (accessed on May 18, 2011).

US Census Bureau. 2007. *2007 Economic Census.* Available at www.census.gov (accessed on June 10, 2011).

US Department of State. 2011. *Supplemental Draft Environmental Impact Statement.* Available at www.keystonepipeline-xl.state.gov (accessed on June 10, 2011).

WCI (Western Climate Initiative). 2008. *Design Recommendations for the WCI Regional Cap-and-Trade Program.* Available at www.westernclimateinitiative.org (accessed on February 27, 2010).

WCI (Western Climate Initiative). 2010. *Design for the WCI Regional Program.* Available at www.westernclimateinitiative.org (accessed on June 10, 2011).

Weintraub, Sidney. 2010. *Unequal Partners: The US and Mexico.* Pittsburgh: University of Pittsburgh Press.

Wiener, Jonathan. 2007. *Think Globally, Act Locally: The Limits of Local Climate Policies.* Duke Law Faculty Scholarship Paper 1623. Available at http://eprints.law.duke.edu/1623.

Wiser, Ryan, and Galen Barbose. 2008. *Renewables Portfolio Standards: A Status Report with Data Through 2007.* Berkeley: Lawrence Berkeley National Laboratory.

Wiser, Ryan, Galen Barbose, and Edward Holt. 2010. *Supporting Solar Power in Renewables Portfolio Standards: Experience from the United States.* Berkeley: Lawrence Berkeley National Laboratory.

Wood, Duncan. 2010. *Environment, Development and Growth: US-Mexico Cooperation in Renewable Energies.* Washington: Woodrow Wilson Center Mexico Institute.

World Bank. 2009. *Program Document for a Proposed Framework for Green Growth Development Policy Loan in the Amount of US$1.504 Billion to the United Mexican States.* Report No. 49491-MX. Washington.

World Bank. 2010. *Project Performance Assessment Report: Mexico: First and Second Community Forestry Projects.* Report No. 55416. Washington.

Acronyms

ACESA	American Clean Energy and Security Act (Waxman-Markey bill)
BACT	best available control technology (US Clean Air Act)
BECC	Border Environment Cooperation Commission
CAFE	corporate average fuel economy standard
CARB	California Air Resources Board
CCS	carbon capture and storage
CDM	Clean Development Mechanism
CEC	Commission for Environmental Cooperation
CFE	Federal Electricity Commission of Mexico
CEPA	Canadian Environmental Protection Act
CO_2e	carbon dioxide equivalent
EPA	US Environmental Protection Agency
EIA	US Energy Information Administration
EITE	energy-intensive, trade-exposed industry
FIT	feed-in tariff
GATT	General Agreement on Tariffs and Trade
GEF	Global Environmental Facility
GHG	greenhouse gas
IDB	Inter-American Development Bank
INE	National Institute of Ecology of Mexico
IPP	independent power producer
LCFS	low-carbon fuel standard
MFN	most favored nation
MRV	monitoring, reporting, and verification
NAAEC	North American Agreement on Environmental Cooperation
NAAQS	National Ambient Air Quality Standards (US Clean Air Act)

NADB	North American Development Bank
NAFTA	North American Free Trade Agreement
NRTEE	National Roundtable on the Environment and the Economy of Canada
NSPS	New Source Performance Standards (US Clean Air Act)
NSR	New Source Review (US Clean Air Act)
OECD	Organization for Economic Cooperation and Development
PEMEX	Petróleos Mexicanos
PECC	Special Climate Change Program of Mexico
PRTR	Pollution Release and Transfer Registry
PSD	Prevention of Significant Deterioration (US Clean Air Act)
REC	renewable electricity certificate
REDD	reduced emissions from deforestation and degradation
RGGI	Regional Greenhouse Gas Initiative
RPS	renewable portfolio standard
Semarnat	Mexican Secretariat of Environment and Natural Resources
SENER	Mexican Secretariat of Energy
UNAM	National Autonomous University of Mexico
UNFCCC	United Nations Framework Convention on Climate Change
USAID	United States Agency for International Development
USITC	United States International Trade Commission
WCI	Western Climate Initiative
WTO	World Trade Organization

Index

Suzuki Foundation, 91, 91n

tariffs
    feed-in, 83–84, 137
    most-favored nation, 85, 85n
technical assistance, for developing countries,
        14–15, 68–69, 130–31, 140–41
terrorist attacks (September 11, 2001), 7, 48
top-down policy development, 22, 128
trade law
    clarification of, 137–40, 144
    GATT, 41–42, 46–47, 65
    WTO (*See* World Trade Organization)
trade-vulnerable industries, Canadian, 95,
        96t–98t
trading allowances. *See* border allowance
        program
transmission capacity, 17, 134–35
    renewable energy, 48, 56, 123–24, 135
transportation
    Canada, 8, 8n
    freight, 129
    GHG emissions from, 43
    Mexico, 14, 109, 112–13, 120–21
    US, 21, 43
Turning the Corner plan (Canada), 8–9, 75–76,
        102, 102n

UN Framework Convention on Climate
        Change (UNFCCC), 20, 102, 107
United States, 21–73
    Agency for International Development, 113
    bilateral talks
        with Canada, 132
        with Mexico, 124, 132
    biofuels policy, 137, 139
    "Buy American" provisions, 138–39
    climate assistance pledges, 130
    electricity generation, 12, 22–23, 27, 30,
        37–43, 52–53, 72–73
    employment effects, 23–27, 24t–26t
    Energy Information Administration, 37n,
        54, 101
    energy-intensive imports, 66, 66t
    EPA (*See* Environmental Protection Agency)

federal initiatives (*See* federal initiatives)
fossil fuel dependency, 12
GHG emissions, 1–3, 2t, 6, 7f
    distribution of, 22–28
infrastructure networks, 17, 48, 56, 135, 144
Keystone XL pipeline, 12n, 45, 103–104
Kyoto Protocol withdrawal, 5–6, 48
lead role of, 21
oil imports, 18, 44–45
protectionism, 16, 19
regional differences in, 12–13, 22–28,
        127–28
    carbon trading regime and, 69–73,
        70t–71t
regional initiatives, 9–10, 30–37
regulatory uncertainty, 4, 55, 57
State Department, 104
state initiatives (*See* state initiatives)
transportation, 21, 43
United States–Gasoline (WTO case), 46n
*United States–Import Prohibition of Certain Shrimp
        and Shrimp Products* (WTO case), 42n, 65

Wall Street Journal, 22
Waxman, Henry. *See* American Clean Energy
        and Security Act
WCI. *See* Western Climate Initiative
Western Climate Initiative (WCI), 9–10, 10t,
        30–31, 78
    carbon leakage, 33–36
    carbon offsets, 36–37
    linking with other initiatives, 134
    as substitute for federal regulations, 55
Western Energy Corridor, 17
wind power
    Mexico, 112–14, 114n, 123
    transmission capacity, 48, 56, 123–24, 135
Wisconsin, oil sands pipeline project to, 45
wood products sector, 95, 96t
World Bank, 112–13, 130
World Resources Institute, 23, 52
World Trade Organization (WTO)
    trade law clarification, 137, 137n
    US federal initiatives and, 65
    US state initiatives and, 36, 41, 42n, 46n

Other Publications from the Peterson Institute for International Economics

WORKS IN PROGRESS

DISTRIBUTORS OUTSIDE THE UNITED STATES

**Australia, New Zealand,
and Papua New Guinea**
D. A. Information Services
648 Whitehorse Road
Mitcham, Victoria 3132, Australia
Tel: 61-3-9210-7777
Fax: 61-3-9210-7788
Email: service@dadirect.com.au
www.dadirect.com.au

India, Bangladesh, Nepal, and Sri Lanka
Viva Books Private Limited
Mr. Vinod Vasishtha
4737/23 Ansari Road
Daryaganj, New Delhi 110002
India
Tel: 91-11-4224-2200
Fax: 91-11-4224-2240
Email: viva@vivagroupindia.net
www.vivagroupindia.com

**Mexico, Central America, South America,
and Puerto Rico**
US PubRep, Inc.
311 Dean Drive
Rockville, MD 20851
Tel: 301-838-9276
Fax: 301-838-9278
Email: c.falk@ieee.org

Asia (*Brunei, Burma, Cambodia, China,
Hong Kong, Indonesia, Korea, Laos, Malaysia,
Philippines, Singapore, Taiwan, Thailand,
and Vietnam*)
East-West Export Books (EWEB)
University of Hawaii Press
2840 Kolowalu Street
Honolulu, Hawaii 96822-1888
Tel: 808-956-8830
Fax: 808-988-6052
Email: eweb@hawaii.edu

Canada
Renouf Bookstore
5369 Canotek Road, Unit 1
Ottawa, Ontario KlJ 9J3, Canada
Tel: 613-745-2665
Fax: 613-745-7660
www.renoufbooks.com

Japan
United Publishers Services Ltd.
1-32-5, Higashi-shinagawa
Shinagawa-ku, Tokyo 140-0002
Japan
Tel: 81-3-5479-7251
Fax: 81-3-5479-7307
Email: purchasing@ups.co.jp
*For trade accounts only. Individuals will find
Institute books in leading Tokyo bookstores.*

Middle East
MERIC
2 Bahgat Ali Street, El Masry Towers
Tower D, Apt. 24
Zamalek, Cairo
Egypt
Tel. 20-2-7633824
Fax: 20-2-7369355
Email: mahmoud_fouda@mericonline.com
www.mericonline.com

United Kingdom, Europe
(*including Russia and Turkey*)**, Africa,
and Israel**
The Eurospan Group
c/o Turpin Distribution
Pegasus Drive
Stratton Business Park
Biggleswade, Bedfordshire
SG18 8TQ
United Kingdom
Tel: 44 (0) 1767-604972
Fax: 44 (0) 1767-601640
Email: eurospan@turpin-distribution.com
www.eurospangroup.com/bookstore

**Visit our website at:
www.piie.com
E-mail orders to:
petersonmail@presswarehouse.com**